796.32309 RUS

Shapiro, Miles

Bill Russell

WITHDRAWN

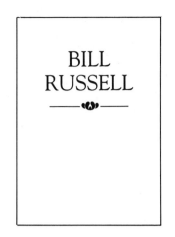

BILL
RUSSELL

BILL RUSSELL

Miles Shapiro

Senior Consulting Editor
Nathan Irvin Huggins
Director
W.E.B. Du Bois Institute for Afro-American Research
Harvard University

CHELSEA HOUSE PUBLISHERS
New York   Philadelphia

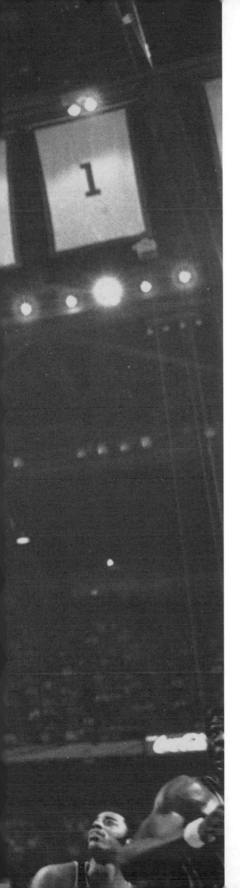

Chelsea House Publishers
Editor-in-Chief Remmel Nunn
Managing Editor Karyn Gullen Browne
Copy Chief Juliann Barbato
Picture Editor Adrian G. Allen
Art Director Maria Epes
Deputy Copy Chief Mark Rifkin
Assistant Art Director Loraine Machlin
Manufacturing Manager Gerald Levine
Systems Manager Lindsey Ottman
Production Manager Joseph Romano
Production Coordinator Marie Claire Cebrián

Black Americans of Achievement
Senior Editor Richard Rennert

Staff for BILL RUSSELL
Copy Editor Philip Koslow
Editorial Assistant Michele Haddad
Picture Researcher Alan Gottlieb
Designer Ghila Krajzman
Cover Illustration Alan J. Nahigian

First Printing

1 3 5 7 9 8 6 4 2

Library of Congress Cataloging-in-Publication Data

Shapiro, Miles.
    Bill Russell/by Miles Shapiro.
        p.   cm.—(Black Americans of achievement)
    Includes bibliographical references.
    Summary: A biography of the outstanding basketball player who
joined the Boston Celtics in the 1956–57 season and led the team to
11 NBA championships in the 13 years he played.
    ISBN 0-7910-1136-4
        0-7910-1161-5 (pbk.)
    1. Russell, Bill, 1934–   —Juvenile literature. 2. Basketball
players—United States—Biography—Juvenile literature. 3. Boston
Celtics (Basketball team)—History—Juvenile literature. [1. Russell,
Bill, 1934– . 2. Basketball players. 3. Afro-Americans—
Biography.] I. Title. II. Series.
GV884.R86S53 1990
796.323'092—dc20   90-35638
[B]   CIP
[92]   AC

Frontispiece: *Bill Russell (6) at
Boston Garden.*

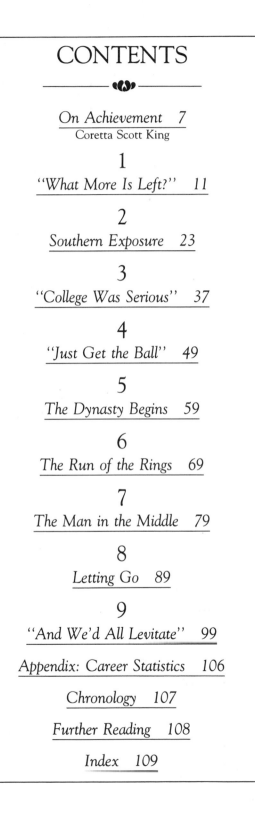

CONTENTS

10/29/91

17.95

B&T

BLACK AMERICANS OF ACHIEVEMENT

RALPH ABERNATHY
civil rights leader

MUHAMMAD ALI
heavyweight champion

RICHARD ALLEN
religious leader and social activist

LOUIS ARMSTRONG
musician

ARTHUR ASHE
tennis great

JOSEPHINE BAKER
entertainer

JAMES BALDWIN
author

BENJAMIN BANNEKER
scientist and mathematician

AMIRI BARAKA
poet and playwright

COUNT BASIE
bandleader and composer

ROMARE BEARDEN
artist

JAMES BECKWOURTH
frontiersman

MARY McLEOD
BETHUNE
educator

BLANCHE BRUCE
politician

RALPH BUNCHE
diplomat

GEORGE WASHINGTON
CARVER
botanist

CHARLES CHESNUTT
author

BILL COSBY
entertainer

PAUL CUFFE
merchant and abolitionist

FATHER DIVINE
religious leader

FREDERICK DOUGLASS
abolitionist editor

CHARLES DREW
physician

W.E.B. DU BOIS
scholar and activist

PAUL LAURENCE DUNBAR
poet

KATHERINE DUNHAM
dancer and choreographer

MARIAN WRIGHT EDELMAN
civil rights leader and lawyer

DUKE ELLINGTON
bandleader and composer

RALPH ELLISON
author

JULIUS ERVING
basketball great

JAMES FARMER
civil rights leader

ELLA FITZGERALD
singer

MARCUS GARVEY
black-nationalist leader

DIZZY GILLESPIE
musician

PRINCE HALL
social reformer

W. C. HANDY
father of the blues

WILLIAM HASTIE
educator and politician

MATTHEW HENSON
explorer

CHESTER HIMES
author

BILLIE HOLIDAY
singer

JOHN HOPE
educator

LENA HORNE
entertainer

LANGSTON HUGHES
poet

ZORA NEALE HURSTON
author

JESSE JACKSON
civil rights leader and politician

JACK JOHNSON
heavyweight champion

JAMES WELDON JOHNSON
author

SCOTT JOPLIN
composer

BARBARA JORDAN
politician

MARTIN LUTHER KING, JR.
civil rights leader

ALAIN LOCKE
scholar and educator

JOE LOUIS
heavyweight champion

RONALD McNAIR
astronaut

MALCOLM X
militant black leader

THURGOOD MARSHALL
Supreme Court justice

ELIJAH MUHAMMAD
religious leader

JESSE OWENS
champion athlete

CHARLIE PARKER
musician

GORDON PARKS
photographer

SIDNEY POITIER
actor

ADAM CLAYTON POWELL, JR.
political leader

LEONTYNE PRICE
opera singer

A. PHILIP RANDOLPH
labor leader

PAUL ROBESON
singer and actor

JACKIE ROBINSON
baseball great

BILL RUSSELL
basketball great

JOHN RUSSWURM
publisher

SOJOURNER TRUTH
antislavery activist

HARRIET TUBMAN
antislavery activist

NAT TURNER
slave revolt leader

DENMARK VESEY
slave revolt leader

MADAME C. J. WALKER
entrepreneur

BOOKER T. WASHINGTON
educator

HAROLD WASHINGTON
politician

WALTER WHITE
civil rights leader and author

RICHARD WRIGHT
author

ON ACHIEVEMENT

Coretta Scott King

BEFORE YOU BEGIN this book, I hope you will ask yourself what the word excellence means to you. I think that it's a question we should all ask, and keep asking as we grow older and change. Because the truest answer to it should never change. When you think of excellence, perhaps you think of success at work; or of becoming wealthy; or meeting the right person, getting married, and having a good family life.

Those important goals are worth striving for, but there is a better way to look at excellence. As Martin Luther King, Jr., said in one of his last sermons, "I want you to be first in love. I want you to be first in moral excellence. I want you to be first in generosity. If you want to be important, wonderful. If you want to be great, wonderful. But recognize that he who is greatest among you shall be your servant."

My husband, Martin Luther King, Jr., knew that the true meaning of achievement is service. When I met him, in 1952, he was already ordained as a Baptist preacher and was working towards a doctoral degree at Boston University. I was studying at the New England Conservatory and dreamed of accomplishments in music. We married a year later, and after I graduated the following year we moved to Montgomery, Alabama. We didn't know it then, but our notions of achievement were about to undergo a dramatic change.

You may have read or heard about what happened next. What began with the boycott of a local bus line grew into a national movement, and by the time he was assassinated in 1968 my husband had fashioned a black movement powerful enough to shatter forever the practice of racial segregation. What you may not have read about is where he got his method for resisting injustice without compromising his religious beliefs.

He adopted the strategy of nonviolence from a man of a different race, who lived in a distant country, and even practiced a different religion. The man was Mahatma Gandhi, the great leader of India, who devoted his life to serving humanity in the spirit of love and nonviolence. It was in these principles that Martin discovered his method for social reform. More than anything else, those two principles were the key to his achievements.

This book is about black Americans who served society through the excellence of their achievements. It forms a part of the rich history of black men and women in America—a history of stunning accomplishments in every field of human endeavor, from literature and art to science, industry, education, diplomacy, athletics, jurisprudence, even polar exploration.

Not all of the people in this history had the same ideals, but I think you will find something that all of them have in common. Like Martin Luther King, Jr., they all decided to become "drum majors" and serve humanity. In that principle—whether it was expressed in books, inventions, or song—they found something outside themselves to use as a goal and a guide. Something that showed them a way to serve others, instead of living only for themselves.

Reading the stories of these courageous men and women not only helps us discover the principles that we will use to guide our own lives but also teaches us about our black heritage and about America itself. It is crucial for us to know the heroes and heroines of our history and to realize that the price we paid in our struggle for equality in America was dear. But we must also understand that we have gotten as far as we have partly because America's democratic system and ideals made it possible.

We are still struggling with racism and prejudice. But the great men and women in this series are a tribute to the spirit of our democratic ideals and the system in which they have flourished. And that makes their stories special and worth knowing.

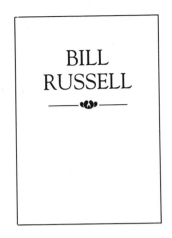

BILL
RUSSELL

1

"WHAT MORE IS LEFT?"

Russell looks to hang yet another championship banner from the Boston Garden rafters as he huddles with his teammates during a time-out at the 1967 National Basketball Association (NBA) playoffs. On his way to revolutionizing the sport of basketball, he helped the Boston Celtics win 8 straight NBA titles and 11 championships in 13 seasons.

HE IS AN unbelievable man."

Those words emerged in the spring of 1968 from the downturned lips of Jerry West, star guard of the Los Angeles Lakers. "They can talk about individual players in any sport, but I tell you what, when it comes to winning, there is no one like him. . . . I play this game, and I know. I know. What has this man won? Ten championships. Ten championships in 12 years. Has there ever been anyone like him?"

The "him" was Bill Russell, the 34-year-old head coach and center of the Boston Celtics. Widely regarded as the greatest defensive player in all of basketball, he had just led his green-and-white-clad teammates against the Philadelphia 76ers and the Lakers in two best-of-seven-games series—the semifinal and final rounds of the 1968 National Basketball Association (NBA) playoffs. The Celtics had relinquished the NBA title the previous year—and indeed it had been theirs: 8 championships in a row, 9 out of the last 10—to the 76ers, powered by the herculean Wilt Chamberlain. That season had been Russell's first as head coach of Boston, and he had experienced a great deal of trouble adjusting to his dual role as player and coach.

"Some of the things he did last year," 76ers head coach Alex Hannum said of Russell's strategy moves during the 1966–67 season, "well, I just had to scratch my head at them." *Sports Illustrated* even referred to one of Russell's coaching maneuvers during the 1967 playoffs as a "gaffe . . . when he apparently forgot that Sam Jones was sitting on the bench in one game"—harsh words from a major sports publication.

No such gaffe occurred during the 1968 playoffs. Even Hannum concurred, "There was none of that this season." Instead, Russell's magnificent play and heady coaching led the Celtics into the Eastern Division finals against the 76ers. Boston won the first contest handily and then dropped the next two, setting up a pivotal fourth game: The Celtics were aware that no team in NBA history had won a seven-game series after being down three games to one.

The Celtics fell behind in Game 4, but they did not panic. Instead, Russell's squad put together a patented comeback in the fourth quarter, closing the gap to 107–101. Unlike past Boston team efforts, however, this one fell short. Hal Greer, the talented 76ers forward, stole an errant Celtics pass and hit two shots in a row, thus squelching Boston's hopes of a come-from-behind victory.

"Russell performed gallantly and so did Sam Jones," the *New York Times* reported. "Each is 34 years old, a tipoff on the decline of the team that ruled the NBA for eight consecutive seasons." The sports world, it seemed, was ready to write off the Russell-led five.

Shockingly, Celtics general manager and former head coach Arnold "Red" Auerbach was among the people who spoke of Russell in the past tense. "There are some people who have already forgotten how great that man really was," an infuriated Auerbach said of Russell's critics after the fourth game of the Philadelphia series. It sounded as though Auerbach too was forgetting that his star player had successfully met every new challenge.

Russell himself believed that neither the series nor his career was over. After all he had accomplished, why should he think so? During the 12 years that he had been with Boston, he had played almost 40,000 minutes in nearly 900 games. He had scored more than 13,000 points, had grabbed more than 20,000 rebounds, and had reshaped the art of defense on Boston's way to winning 9 league championships. In each of his campaigns, he had been cited as either a first- or second-team all-NBA performer. He had been named the league's most valuable player an unprecedented five times.

Nevertheless, Russell knew it would take the entirety of his gifts to guide his team to victory in three straight games over a foe as talented as the Philadelphia 76ers. He was not the league's top scoring threat. That title belonged to Wilt Chamberlain, who made baskets seemingly at will. (The Big Dipper, as Chamberlain was also known, stood 3 inches taller than the 6-foot-10-inch Russell and outweighed him by more than 50 pounds.) And Russell was no longer the NBA's leading rebounder. San Francisco Warriors center Nate Thurmond, for one, was broader and stronger than Russell and pulled down more rebounds.

At age 34, Russell was probably not even the best player on his own team, whose roster included Wayne Embry, Don Nelson, Thomas "Satch" Sanders, and Larry Siegfried. John Havlicek, Bailey Howell, and Sam Jones usually led the Boston attack. Yet no one helped the team win more than Russell. He was always the common denominator for the Celtics' success.

Whereas most players looked to put the ball in the basket, Russell did not care about how many

Russell confers with Arnold "Red" Auerbach, the mastermind behind Boston's rise to the top of the NBA. At the end of the 1965–66 season, Auerbach retired as head coach of the Celtics and named the 32-year-old Russell as his replacement.

points he scored (even though he tallied more points in his career than all but 14 other NBA players). Instead, he concentrated on other aspects of the game. Although his passing skills were not equal to those of his legendary teammate Bob Cousy or those of Oscar Robertson of the Cincinnati Royals, Russell was a very fine passing center—better than most who played the position. He also snared over his career an average of more than 22 rebounds per game, an accomplishment requiring not just size and jumping ability but an understanding of how to position oneself beneath the basket as well as a keen sense of anticipation and timing. Only the mammoth Chamberlain has ever averaged more rebounds.

But it was on defense, the aspect of basketball that is not well served by statistical analysis, that Russell shone brighter than any other star in the league. Able to jump high and quickly and possessing fabulous foot speed for a man of his size, he became the game's most feared shot blocker. "What you try to do," he wrote in his autobiography *Second Wind*, "is to intimidate your opponent with the idea that you *might* block any shot." Russell felt he could block about 10 shots per game. "Knowing which shots to go after is one of the most difficult arts in defensive basketball," he said, "and it contributes a great deal to winning games."

Russell also knew how to inspire his teammates to attain their goals. An intense competitor, he maintained a single-mindedness on the court that allowed him to pursue the ball bouncing off the rim, to fight through screens, to shoot the ball, and to defend his basket with a fury that always seemed to produce success; yet Russell's concentration was never so focused that he was unable to incorporate complicated strategies into his game. Clearly, it was his fine basketball mind—his disciplined approach to the sport and his understanding of how it should be played—

that separated him from every other center in the league.

When the savvy Red Auerbach retired as coach of the Celtics in 1966, after 16 years at the helm, he decided boldly that instead of leaving the team in the hands of someone exactly like most other NBA coaches—a conventional strategist, older than the players, and white—the right man for the job had been in the Boston huddle since 1956. Russell thus became the youngest coach in the league—and the first black to coach a team in any modern major professional sport.

The high-scoring Wilt Chamberlain (right) goes up against Russell, the NBA's most dominating defensive player ever. Combining strength and size with balletic grace, these two giants of the game formed the league's most exciting rivalry.

EXTREMELY FAMILIAR WITH tough situations and accustomed to winning, Russell approached Game 5 against Philadelphia with his characteristic intelligence and singleness of purpose. Being on the brink of elimination against the defending champions did not faze him. Instead, Russell and the Celtics went about their work diligently as more than 15,000 hostile 76ers fans rooted for the visiting team's demise. The result: Boston trounced the 76ers, 122–104.

Although Russell netted only 8 points in the game, he dominated the defensive backboard, grabbing 24 rebounds. Philadelphia coach Hannum declared, "Every rebound was theirs."

Russell shrugged off his team's lopsided victory. He would only say that the Celtics had finally returned to "defensive fundamentals." When someone asked him what he had told his players in his pregame talk, Russell responded, "I didn't say anything inspirational. I'm not that type of guy."

What type of guy Russell was came clearly into focus in Game 6. He scored 17 points and grabbed an astounding 31 rebounds, enabling the Celtics to waltz by the startled 76ers and tie the series at 3 games apiece.

Yet the odds were still against Boston, who had to play the final game on Philadelphia's home court. "History favors the 76ers," the *New York Times* stated on April 17. "The Celtics once trailed in the series 3–1 and no NBA team has ever rallied from that deficit to win a four-of-seven-game series playoff."

But history was about to be rewritten. "Russell, as brilliant as ever," Frank Deford wrote the following week in *Sports Illustrated*, "restricted Chamberlain in a manner few believed possible. In the last half of the critical final game Wilt took only one shot." But that was not all the Celtics player-coach did. With the clock winding down, Boston's lead was a scant 2 points, 97–95. That was when Russell, one of the "old men" referred to on a painted bedsheet banner held up by one of the Philadelphia faithful, took over the game. With 32 seconds left to play, he hit a foul shot. Then he blocked Wali Jones's shot at the other end of the court. When Hal Greer missed a follow-up jumper, Russell snared the rebound, thus securing the game—and the Eastern Division title—for the Celtics.

The Los Angeles Lakers, the Western Division champions, had been waiting patiently for a week for a winner to emerge from the Boston-Philadelphia series. Led by two of the game's best all-around players, Jerry West and Elgin Baylor, Los Angeles had completely dominated the San Francisco Warriors in their semifinal matchup. Thanks to their four-game sweep, the Lakers were a well-rested and well-prepared team going into the final round. And they were confident they could beat Boston.

"If we can rebound," West said, "we can win. We're little, but we match up well with Boston. We're quick and we shoot well, and that can be enough in a seven-game series."

Russell loomed as the key to it all. It was his responsibility, more than any of his teammates', to control the backboards and stall the Los Angeles attack. If he could manage to do those things, Boston would have a good shot at recapturing the title.

In the first game of the championship series, the Lakers welcomed the Celtics to the NBA finals by pushing them around the court for the first 2 quarters of play; Boston trailed at halftime by 13 points. As the Celtics sat dejectedly in their locker room during the 10-minute intermission, Russell did not yell at his troops and tell them they were playing terribly. Instead, he spoke calmly. He said the Celtics were not executing their plays efficiently enough to defeat the gifted Lakers. He implored his teammates to run their plays crisply, "on a straight line, instead of a half-circle."

The Celtics proved to be dutiful students under Professor Russell's tutelage. The Lakers could not make a shot during a dismal stretch in the fourth quarter, and Boston left the arena with a 107–101 victory. Russell again dominated the backboards, grabbing 25 rebounds; he scored 19 points as well. Still, it was his ability to distance himself from the action and assess his team's problems in the first half that had turned the game around.

Game 2 was a different story. Jerry West scored 35 points, and his partner in crime, Elgin Baylor, tallied 23 as Los Angeles skipped by a tired Celtics team that at last showed the effects of going from the semifinal series to the finals without a layoff.

After Boston and Los Angeles split their next two meetings, knotting the series at two games apiece, the action shifted back to the Lakers' home court.

Game 5 was the gem of the series. The contest, held on April 30, was tight throughout and went into overtime. Then, toward the end of the extra session, a spectacular defensive feat helped determine the outcome of the game. Predictably, this trick was turned by the greatest defensive player of all time.

Boston had just taken the lead, 119–117, when Baylor, with less than 30 seconds remaining, drove to his left and went up for a quick jump shot close to the basket. It was a routine move for the high-scoring Baylor, one of the sport's all-time greats—a nearly automatic two points on the board.

Russell appeared to be nowhere near the play. But all at once he came flying across the foul lane, his 6-foot-10-inch frame extended to the limit. One of his long, sinewy arms batted the ball out of the air and into the hands of a teammate, and the Lakers' chance to tie the game disappeared. Don Nelson drew a foul at the other end of the court; he made 1 of 2 free

Russell bats the ball away from Archie Clark of the Los Angeles Lakers during a key moment in Game 5 of the 1968 NBA finals. No player in NBA history has ever defended his team's basket more staunchly than Russell did.

throws to clinch the 120–117 victory, which again gave Boston a 1-game lead.

The Lakers hoped to even up the series at Boston Garden. But Game 6 proved to be anticlimactic; the series finale was a rout. Havlicek scored 40 points, and his running mate, Bailey Howell, got 30. With the Celtics leading by 21 points midway through the fourth quarter, Russell, not wishing to embarrass his opponents, pulled himself and the other starters from the floor and let the substitutes finish the lopsided 124–109 Boston victory.

A familiar sight to basketball fans during the late 1950s and 1960s: Russell and his mentor, Red Auerbach, celebrate a Boston victory. During Russell's professional career, the Celtics posted a 703 and 296 record during the regular season.

The Celtics were once again NBA champions, earning the title for the 9th time in the last 10 years and the 10th time in the last 12. But now Russell could celebrate twice, both as a player and as the architect of his team's triumph. "What more is left for him to achieve in his sport?" *Sports Illustrated* asked.

Russell's reply told a lot about him. Rather than trumpet his double achievement, he said: "Well, I don't know, because I never had a goal. To tell you the truth, it's been a long time since I tried to prove anything to anybody. *I* know who I am."

And who Bill Russell is, is a winner. Indeed, no other player in basketball history has ever been the key to as many championship teams as he has. From the fall of 1956 to the spring of 1969, the Boston Celtics were the most dominant professional team to play *any* sport *ever*. It is no coincidence those are the same years that Russell was with the club. Not even the New York Yankees, led in the late 1920s and early 1930s by all-time baseball greats Babe Ruth and Lou Gehrig, or the Montreal Canadiens hockey team, winners of six Stanley Cups during the 1950s, ever ruled an era in sports the way the Celtics did under Russell.

Along with the record number of league titles he won with the Celtics, Russell was also the starting center and focal point for the U.S. Olympic basketball team that won the gold medal in 1956 and for the University of San Francisco (USF) squads that won both the 1955 and 1956 National Collegiate Athletic Association (NCAA) basketball championships. His college team also held the national record for most consecutive games won: 60 (with 5 of the wins coming after Russell's senior year), until coach John Wooden assembled his standout ball clubs at the University of California at Los Angeles (UCLA) almost a decade later. These different accomplishments have led the nation's sportswriters to cite Russell as the greatest player in basketball history and many people to call him the top winner in all of sports.

Russell's brilliance as a basketball performer and tactician is usually attributed to his extraordinary physical gifts and acute intelligence. But there are other explanations for his phenomenal success, and they all point back to Monroe, Louisiana, where Bill Russell passed his first nine years. ✿

2

SOUTHERN
EXPOSURE

W ILLIAM FELTON RUSSELL'S introduction
into the world lacked the fanfare and expectations
that would later accompany the basketball star's every
step. He was born on February 12, 1934, in Monroe,
Louisiana, a small industrial city located in the
swampy southeastern portion of the state. Founded
in 1785 as a small outpost on the banks of the Ouachita River, Fort Miro (as the town was originally
known) changed its name to Fort Monroe in 1820
to celebrate the passage of the first steamship to travel
up the Ouachita, the *James Monroe*. The town's name
was shortened to its current form in 1900, when Monroe became a municipality.

By the time Bill was born 34 years later, Monroe
had developed into a typical city in the Deep South,
a place where racial segregation determined the pat-
terns of life and blacks were treated as second-class
citizens. Whites managed to keep blacks "in their
place" and bar them from using white facilities and
institutions through Jim Crow laws, local statutes that
enforced racial separation.

Nevertheless, it took several years before Bill's
view of the world was colored by these discriminatory
practices. "When you're a kid, you just never realize
that there is a tremendous basic difference between

*The future basketball star at age
five, near his home in Monroe,
Louisiana. According to Russell,
"Growing up in the Deep South
did not have as disturbing an
effect" on him as when he visited
there as an adult and saw racial
oppression everywhere he went.*

mere existence and freedom," Russell wrote in his autobiography *Go Up for Glory*. "I was just a kid who liked his friends and loved his mother and father and brother and scuffed along the dirt road, laughing, on my way to a barn that was converted into a school."

Bill developed a strong sense of security from being part of a tightly knit family. His father, whom Bill and everyone else called Mister Charlie, delighted in coming home from his job at a paper-bag factory and having his wife and two sons join him in a nearby field for a game of hide-and-seek. Charlie Russell was a huge, fun-loving man of unbending strength. Revered by Monroe's black community, he was very much his own person: full of pride and willing to stand up to anyone, including his white boss, when the situation arose. According to Bill, "Charlie Russell was not a man who was ever going to be kept back."

Bill's mother, the former Katie King, was equally strong willed and warmhearted. Whenever Charlie Russell failed to display much outward affection to Bill and his older brother, Charlie, their mother more than made up for it, especially as far as Bill was concerned. A sickly child—particularly during infancy, when he developed pneumonia twice—he required her constant attention. "Everbody knew that Katie Russell was sweet on me, and she stood by me like this fierce guardian," he recalled in *Second Wind*.

Bill's character was also molded by his paternal grandfather, a champion logroller and woodsman who performed odd jobs for a living. Bill loved nothing more during his Louisiana boyhood than to spend time with the elder Russell. Known as the Old Man, Bill's grandfather was just as strong and tough as Bill's father. According to the young Russell, "The Old Man never worked for anyone" and "never kowtowed to anybody." One afternoon, an astonished Bill watched his grandfather knock out an especially stubborn mule with a single blow.

When left to his own devices, Bill made his own fun. Fascinated by trains, he liked to sit along the tracks near his home and wave to the engineers as the railroad cars chugged by. He also enjoyed joking around with his brother. On one memorable occasion, he and Charlie snuck out of bed and, blanketed by white sheets, hid outside their house to frighten a visiting couple who believed in ghosts.

Bill was also encouraged by his parents to spend a good deal of his time studying, for Charlie and Katie Russell continually stressed the importance of an education. In fact, in 1935—just a year after Bill's birth and a time when most blacks in America could not afford to study at a university—Bill's parents began to save their money with the hope that one day they would be able to send the boys to college.

Most of the people Bill encountered at his one-room schoolhouse and just about everywhere else in Monroe were black. "The white kids I did see usually threw rocks at my friends and me when we walked into town," he said in *Second Wind*. On several occasions, he saw his parents treated discourteously by whites.

The last time he witnessed such a scene in the South was in the spring of 1943, when Bill and his brother were driving home with their father, who stopped for gas at a local station. The white attendant paid no attention to them, however; he serviced other cars and chatted with the white customers. When Bill's father decided not to wait any longer and prepared to drive away, the gas station attendant grabbed a rifle and ran over to the automobile, then started to yell at Charlie Russell for not being more respectful to whites. Unwilling to take that kind of abuse from anyone, Mister Charlie grabbed a tire iron and went after him. The worker immediately turned on his heels and fled.

Although their father's bold action thrilled the boys, it did not cheer Charlie Russell; he decided the

time had come for him and his family to move away from Monroe. He immediately made plans to scout another part of the country, which he hoped would be more welcoming to blacks than the Deep South was.

First, Charlie Russell went to Detroit, where he found a job in an automobile factory. But before he sent for his family, he realized that he could not tolerate the cold northern winter. A short time later, he headed for the warmer climate of California, eventually settling in Oakland. As soon as he landed a

Racial segregation was a way of life in Monroe, a small industrial center located in northern Louisiana. Russell scarcely had any contact with white society in this southern city, where he spent his first nine years before moving to Oakland, California.

decent job and a place to live, he told his family to join him.

At the age of nine, Bill said good-bye to Louisiana and moved with his mother and brother to the West Coast. Unlike the many prospectors who had streamed to California in search of gold a century earlier, the Russells were simply looking for a good, solid life.

The first place they lived in the Bay Area was an eight-room house, which they shared with eight other families. This home was located at the northern end of Oakland, in an area aptly called Landlord's Paradise. A short time after that, the Russells moved into a West Oakland "integrated" project, a group of apartments where whites lived in one section and blacks in another. Their apartment building was situated close to the Cole School, the elementary school that Bill attended, and it was in the project yard that he first played the game of basketball.

For a brief period, Bill's parents viewed California with the attitude of a miner who pans for gold and finds a small chunk of the precious metal: not enough to make him rich but enough to make the trip worthwhile. Both Charlie Russell and his wife landed jobs in the local shipyard. Then Mister Charlie established a small trucking business that helped ease his family's financial burden.

"Oakland, compared with Louisiana," Russell wrote in *Go Up for Glory*, "was Paradise gained." Living on the West Coast seemed to benefit him greatly as he grew from a small child into a tall teenager. Those years of growth did not click off, however, with the incremental precision of a timepiece. Rather, there were many starts and stops and lessons to be learned.

As always, Bill's mother was his best teacher. Happy to be attending a school that had real desks and a teacher for every grade, he remained an eager student. His mother, pleased by Bill's industriousness, was always quick to help him with his lessons. Because of her encouragement, he believed he was capable of accomplishing almost anything.

Along with building up her younger son's confidence, Katie Russell insisted that Bill stand up for himself. One day in 1943, she watched another boy slap him in the project yard. When she realized that Bill was not going to defend himself, she collared him and made him square off against his attacker. In the meantime, another youth shouted an insult at Bill.

As soon as the ruckus ended, Katie Russell made Bill fight the second boy, too.

Bill faced his stiffest challenge in the fall of 1946, after he returned home from school one day to discover that his mother had been hospitalized. He was told there was nothing to worry about; she simply had a severe case of the flu. Bill visited her often at the hospital throughout the next two weeks. Then the worst imaginable thing happened. Mister Charlie woke up his two sons in the middle of the night and told them, "Your mother died tonight."

A few days later, a devastated Bill accompanied his father and brother on a train to Monroe, where the body of Katie Russell was to be laid to rest. It was a long ride from California to Louisiana, and Charlie Russell's silence dominated the trip, which was punctuated by several visits to the baggage car, where he and his sons stared solemnly at the casket. The funeral in Monroe attracted all their relatives, but Bill's memory of the event is limited to his refusal to view his mother's body in the open coffin.

The day after the funeral, Bill's father and his kin discussed the future of the Russell boys. Most of their relatives felt Mister Charlie would not be able to raise two boys on his own and expected him to return to the family fold in Monroe, where he could be given a helping hand. When Bill's father said he was going back to Oakland, the clan believed he would be traveling there by himself; they simply could not imagine a man holding down a job and bringing up two boys at the same time. But that is exactly what Charlie Russell had in mind.

On the ride back to California, he gave his boys a rousing pep talk. "We gonna cook. We gonna wash dishes. We gonna get along," he told them. "And remember, I've got to work. When I come home I'm gonna be half hot anyway, and I don't want to be raising hell with you about nothing. We gonna wash our clothes. We gonna keep our bed clean. We gonna live like *people*. And you two gonna get an education."

According to Bill, "That dose of Mister Charlie's intensity lasted for a long time." The boys cooked and cleaned to the best of their ability. The many hours during which they performed their household chores were more than matched by the enormous sacrifice their father made. He gave up his profitable trucking business, whose long hours had often kept him away from the apartment, and took a lower-paying job in a foundry so he could spend more of his time looking after his children.

Bill continued to feel the sting of his mother's absence, but only once, when catching a fatherly scolding, did he rely on the self-pitying excuse that he had no mother. On that occasion, Mister Charlie boomed back in anger that *he* did not have one either.

This exchange did little to comfort Bill, however. He had always gushed with confidence with his mother at his side. Now he felt cheated out of life's possibilities. "It was no secret that I wasn't quite the same person, and people said so," he recalled. Instead of passing the time with his friends, he became deeply introverted, all the while relying more heavily on his father than ever before.

As Bill began to withdraw, he turned to the world of books. A library card soon emerged as one of his most prized possessions, and "We could look it up" became his frequent cry during disputes with his brother. Bill proved to be an especially avid reader of history.

One of the people he liked to read about was Henri Christophe, who helped lead a black revolt on the French colony of St. Domingue, which in 1804 became Haiti, the world's first black republic. Bill was mesmerized by the story of how Christophe crowned himself emperor and built a magnificent fortress-palace in the country's rugged interior.

After failing to make any of the sports teams at Hoover Junior High, Russell served as mascot of the McClymonds High School Warriors before he finally made the school's junior varsity basketball squad in the 10th grade. His decision to play sports was due in part to his wish to follow in the footsteps of his older brother, Charlie, who was an outstanding high school athlete.

The reclusive 13 year old found the Haitian leader's forceful character especially appealing, and Christophe became Bill's favorite hero. Christophe was someone who would not let the world hold him back; his belief that he could achieve anything he desired echoed the words that Bill's mother had often told him.

Christophe's bold refusal to be a slave also struck a deep chord. "His life brought home to me for the first time that being black was not just a limited feeling," Russell wrote in *Second Wind*. Nevertheless, Bill still felt at odds with the world—he believed that the problems he was having were his own fault. While walking along Oakland's streets, he was often stopped and questioned by white policemen who peppered him with racial slurs and told him he was worthless. "It put me in such a state," he said, "that I would shrivel up inside and think, 'Oh, God. They're right.' "

Possessing such an attitude did not get Bill very far. He failed to make any of the sports teams he tried out for at Hoover Junior High School; he could not even manage to make the cheerleading squad. These unsuccessful efforts stood in stark contrast to his brother's achievements. Charlie was a star high school athlete.

By the time Bill was 16 and a student at Mc-Clymonds High School, it seemed he could not sink any lower. And then he suddenly turned his life around. He was walking down the hallway in school one day when he decided it was all right to be who he was; there was no reason to think there was anything wrong with himself. To Bill Russell, this realization was like a religious experience. "From that day on, whenever I've felt hostility from someone, I've assumed that it was their problem rather than mine," he said. "My cowering look turned into a glowering one."

This newfound confidence went nowhere for a while. Then George Powles, a teacher at Mc-Clymonds and the recently appointed coach of the school's junior varsity basketball team, came into Russell's life. "I was clearly the worst of the candidates," Russell said of his tryout for the junior varsity. Yet Powles, who had jerseys for only 15 players, found a way to avoid cutting Bill from the squad. Russell made the team as the 16th man and alternated wearing a uniform every other game with another player.

By his own admission, Powles was not a basketball coach. But he was a fine psychologist and was well liked by the students, an oddity in an all-black school with a predominantly white teaching staff. Powles worked closely with Russell as much as he could and even gave him some money to join a local gym.

Having fallen in love with the sport, Russell spent countless hours teaching himself the rudiments of the game. He was terrific at drills that solely required running and jumping. Basketball, however, is played with a ball, and when that was thrown into the mix, he had his problems. Nevertheless, he moved up to the varsity team during his junior year of high school. Fortunately for Russell, so did Powles.

Although Russell improved game by game, by his senior year he was still, by his own admission, nothing more than a mediocre player. Yet he was part of an excellent high school team, and he benefited in a surprising way from McClymonds's winning record. Instead of graduating in the spring of 1952, Russell finished up in school that January, a time in the year when Brick Swegle, a local basketball lover, traditionally put together a team of California high school all-stars to tour the Pacific Northwest. Russell, now 6 feet 5 inches tall and weighing 160 pounds, was

Russell's high school basketball coach, George Powles (top left), poses with future baseball great Frank Robinson (top right) and the other four starters on McClymonds's 1952 basketball squad. "Our team was excellent, but I was mediocre at best," Russell said. "I was the kind of player who tried so hard that everybody wanted to give me the 'most improved' award—except that I didn't improve much."

Russell's 1952 high school graduation photo. That January, shortly after he graduated from McClymonds High, he left Oakland to tour the Pacific Northwest with a team of California high school all-stars—an experience that gave him an opportunity to improve his game dramatically.

asked to join the 1952 squad chiefly because few players in the Oakland area graduated from school in January and were available to travel up and down the coast to play the local teams.

Like the McClymonds players, the California all-stars took jump shots, a recent development in the game, and left their feet on defense, even though such tactics were frowned upon in most basketball circles in the 1950s. This jumping all over the court was considered "Negro basketball." But Swegle, whose team of all-stars featured only two blacks, wanted his players to have fun on the court, even if it meant resorting to playground-style ball.

Russell learned as much as he could from his teammates. Bill Treu, the best of the all-star players, helped him improve his ball-handling skills and taught him some moves. Eural McKelvey explained to him the art of rebounding, including how to anticipate in which direction a missed shot would bounce. When Russell was on the bench and those two were in the game, he often sat and watched their every move, then tried to picture himself making the exact same movements. At first, he was only able to catch a few steps or an isolated fake—not the entire action. But the next time Treu or McKelvey made the same play, Russell would notice a bit more, then piece the sequence of moves together.

One night, as Russell sat on the bench, he spent a lot of time envisioning the way McKelvey grabbed a particular kind of offensive rebound and put the ball back in the basket. Shortly after Russell got into the game, he snared a rebound and put it right in, just like McKelvey had done. The play left him elated, and he began to introduce more moves into his game. As he ran down the court after each move, he would reflect on the thoroughness of his technique. As it turned out, he was improving not just his basketball skills but his mental discipline.

Russell worked at these moves in practice as well as during games. He realized that he could not duplicate some of the smaller Treu's ball-handling skills (nor, as someone who played close to the basket, was it even wise for him to practice them), so instead of picturing himself executing Treu's moves, he imagined what it would be like to play against Treu and block his shot. Russell took special pleasure in envisioning himself as a defensive player because no one had taught him this knack of imagining himself as someone's counterpart—it was entirely his own discovery.

In the 1950s, most basketball experts thought the key to a winning team was a potent offense—not a tough defense, which is a hallmark of today's top teams. Accordingly, few players worked exceptionally hard on the defensive end of the floor. But Russell turned the game around. Because he felt awkward handling the ball and trying to score points, he became determined to shine on defense, where he could put his exceptional ability to run and jump to good use. He would rebound the ball and block shots, and block them in such a way that either he or a teammate could recover the ball.

As the all-star team wove its way through the Pacific Northwest and into Canada, Russell added to his repertoire daily. When his teammates let him know that he had fashioned a game unlike anyone else's—no one blocked shots like he did—Russell felt he was finally beginning to develop a bit of a reputation as a ballplayer. That feeling made him a much more confident athlete than he had been at Mc-Clymonds, and he was eager to let it be known. As soon as he returned home from the tour, the 18 year old said excitedly to his father, "I can play now!"

But not even Russell realized he would soon become one of the nation's top players. ❧

3

"COLLEGE WAS SERIOUS"

W HEN BILL RUSSELL returned home to Oakland in early 1952, his father told him an exciting piece of news: A man had called while Bill was touring with the California all-stars and wanted to know if the McClymonds High School graduate had any interest in attending college on a scholarship. Going to a university had been a dream of Bill's and his father's for many years. But college was too expensive; they had not saved enough money to send him to school.

Russell realized it was unrealistic to wait for this mysterious caller to phone again and arrange to put him through college, so he applied for a civil service job and became an apprentice sheet-metal worker in the San Francisco Naval Yard. But he did not stop playing basketball. After work, he would go to the local playgrounds and take part in pickup games.

Day by day, Russell's game continued to grow. Moves that he had made in the past with the hesitancy of a colt's first steps were now becoming second nature to him. His physical gifts seemed to blossom as well. His leaping ability began to amaze even himself.

Before long, Russell began to dominate the pickup games with his defense. But excelling on the play-

A high-flying Russell helps the University of San Francisco (USF) Dons extend their record winning streak. Backed by Russell's play, his college team ultimately established a national mark with 55 consecutive wins.

ground was not the same as playing well in organized ball, so be became quite nervous when Hal DeJulio, a former player at the University of San Francisco, called again about the possibility of arranging a basketball scholarship. DeJulio had seen Russell play only once before, at a game in January against Oakland High School, when the teenage center had his best game in a McClymonds uniform. Russell had scored 14 points in the contest and had impressed the alumni scout with his defense. But that performance was not reason enough for the university to offer Russell a scholarship. First, he had to attend a tryout held by USF coach Phil Woolpert.

Russell had never heard of the University of San Francisco. He thought "the University" meant San Francisco State, another school located in the Bay Area. But he soon learned otherwise.

The audition was scheduled to take place in a high school gym because USF did not have its own facility. Russell got lost on his way to the tryout and arrived late. His excitement over this tremendous opportunity and his embarrassment about not being on time left him nervous and a bit tentative as the practice session got under way, yet he soon went all out. At the end of an hour, Coach Woolpert thanked Russell for trying so hard and suggested he take a college entrance examination in the event that he was granted a scholarship. Uncertain that it would be offered to him, Russell returned to Oakland and resumed his routine of working at his sheet-metal job and playing ball on the neighborhood courts.

In March, Russell took part in a game that pitted the McClymonds alumni against the school's varsity team. He displayed his newly developed skills that evening and thoroughly dominated the action. But what he enjoyed most about the evening was the time he went up for a shot and realized he was looking down at the basket. He missed the shot badly, yet his excitement over being that high in the air was so great he could scarcely concentrate for the rest of the game.

In attaining such heights on his jumps, Russell began to fear for his safety: When he was up in the air, it was a long way—more than four feet—to the ground. He quickly got over his worries but not over the joyous sensation he felt when vaulting so high: His fingers were able to reach a spot on the backboard 14 feet above the floor (4 feet higher than the rim). He began to feel a sense of uniqueness that he had reserved in his mind for majestic figures such as Henri Christophe.

Russell felt even more special when he received a letter announcing that he had been awarded a scholarship to USF. The prospect of going to college, as his mother had always wanted him to do, stunned Bill and his father. They found it difficult to believe that DeJulio's unsolicited phone call had actually led to an offer of a free education at a major university. Because Russell did not regard the many hours he had spent perfecting his game as work, he could not interpret the scholarship offer as his just reward. Instead, the chance to earn a college degree struck him as a gift from heaven.

Nevertheless, Russell planned to make the most of this glorious opportunity. He did not view the offer from USF merely as a chance to play organized basketball. In the 1950s, basketball programs at large universities did not lead to lucrative television contracts and large sums of money for the schools, as college basketball does today. Nor did they guarantee national celebrity for star players and certain advancement to the pro ranks. To Russell's way of thinking, college ball was "an extracurricular activity," just like high school basketball had been. "Basketball was play," he said. "College was serious."

A small Jesuit school, USF paid for Russell's tuition, books, and room and board. The college also found a job for him as a dishwasher because the schol-

K. C. Jones, a standout guard at USF, was also Russell's college roommate and close friend. After suiting up for the Dons from 1952 to 1956, they played together on the Boston Celtics for nine years.

arship did not include any spending money. His roommate during that first year was sophomore K. C. Jones, who was also a basketball player on scholarship and seemed just as shy as Russell was. Jones barely said hello to his roommate for nearly a month and would offer him only a nod as he left the room. But one day they finally managed to break the ice, and after that they became inseparable. Jones, who was in possession of a more generous scholarship than Russell was, selflessly shared with his new friend the small sum of money he received from the school for entertainment and clothing expenses.

The two had much in common, above all a love of basketball. They talked about the sport almost to the exclusion of everything else. Both shared a passion for the intricacies of the game, particularly defense. They conversed about blind spots in the eye, peripheral vision, the science of jumping, and other topics usually associated with anatomy and physics, not athletics.

Russell and Jones discovered that an opponent dribbling the ball was more likely to have it stolen when the defender did not position himself directly in front of the player but just off to the side, where the defender's movements could not be as easily detected. Jones mastered this technique and employed it often. The two roommates also performed exercises to improve their own peripheral vision, which enabled them to take in more of the court. And they worked at finding spots on the floor where their opponents would screen each other out, thereby freeing Russell or Jones for a shot or a rebound.

The two turned an extremely physical game into a game for thinkers. Their discussions led them to the discovery that one should not try to block a shot by jumping out at the shooter, because such a maneuver usually took the defender away from where the ball was going and increased his chances of committing a foul with his body. Instead, the defender should jump straight up and extend his arms toward the shooter; this tactic eliminated body contact— and the chance of a foul being called by the officials— and enabled the defender to retain his balance when he landed on the floor, making it easier for him to rebound the ball.

In training himself to jump straight up, Russell also improved his ability to reach over a person who was blocking him out for a rebound. Watching the game closely, he came to realize that about 75 percent of all rebounds were being snared *below* the rim.

USF coaches Ross Guidice (above) and Phil Woolpert (opposite page) helped mold Russell into a topflight basketball player. But it was Russell himself who determined that he should concentrate, he said, "on learning everything I could about defense—and about blocking shots."

Jumping straight up created a tremendous advantage for a player like himself, who could grab the ball well above the basket.

Ross Guidice, who headed the freshman basketball team, was Russell's first coach at USF. A dedicated basketball man, he spent hundreds of hours with Russell after practice, sometimes staying past midnight to teach his young center low-post moves and team concepts he had never learned before. Guidice was able to work with Russell for so many hours because the freshman had a fierce desire to improve his game.

Together, they developed Russell into a very fine college basketball player. Russell was usually quick to notice impatience in others, but he failed to detect a hint of annoyance from his coach. Guidice never once indicated that he was investing too much time on Russell's game. The coach taught his protégé how to set screens and what kinds of passes to throw. He even showed Russell how to shoot a hook shot, which became a staple of his game later in his career.

Russell's freshman team enjoyed a very successful season, winning 19 games and losing only 4. He moved up to the varsity squad the following year, when he was 19. By this time, he had grown to his full 6 feet 10 inches. "Everybody, including me, sensed that there might be something special about the way I was developing as a player," he said in *Second Wind.* Russell continued to develop with the help of Guidice, who doubled as an assistant coach of the varsity club.

By earning a spot as a starting member of the varsity team during his sophomore year, Russell finally got his chance to team up with K. C. Jones in the fall of 1953. The USF Dons opened the season against the heavily favored UCLA Bruins. But with Russell scoring 23 points and blocking 13 shots, the Dons came away with the victory.

What appeared to be a promising season quickly turned sour when Jones suffered a ruptured appendix after the opening game. The illness caused him to miss the rest of the season, and the Dons showed they were not as solid a unit without him on the floor. The team wound up with a 14 and 7 record.

Neverthless, Russell's sophomore season marked a turning point in his development as a player. The biggest change in his game took place during the early part of the schedule, in a meeting with Brigham Young University. The Dons team captain, a white player who resented the attention Russell received from Coach Woolpert, had made it a habit to criticize the sophomore center whenever the opportunity arose. After the first play of the game against Brigham Young, during which the opposing center had dribbled around Russell and put in a layup, the USF captain demanded of his own center, "Why don't you try playing some defense?"

Russell lost his cool. All he would do for the rest of the game, he decided, was play defense. He spent the entire first half making sure that his man did not even touch the ball, let alone score another point, even though it meant not helping out his own teammates on defense. He did not shoot the ball or set picks to free other players for open shots. But on defense he played like a man possessed.

During halftime, Woolpert dressed Bill down in front of his teammates, asking him what he was trying to prove. At that moment, a seething Russell decided to put everything he had into playing great basketball. When he returned to the court, he took over the game. And he continued to play in a frenzy for the next ball game and the game after that. "I made up my mind to be a championship basketball player" was his explanation for his transformation from a mere star into the most impressive type of athlete, a consistent winner.

The transformation came about because Russell learned an important lesson during his sophomore year: Teams win, not individuals. Although the Dons in 1953 were an exceptionally talented team, they finished the season with a mediocre record because each player went his own way. Russell perceived this so clearly that he was able to draw on it for the rest of his career.

By 1954, the Dons were ready to play together as a team should. Strengthened by the return of the ball-hawking Jones and the graduation of the previous year's more selfish players, the USF squad opened the season with convincing wins over Chico State and Loyola Marymount University. Next, the Dons faced UCLA and its all-American center, Willie Naulls. Russell blanketed Naulls, but the Bruins won the hard-fought contest, 47–40.

The tough loss against a first-rate squad had a positive effect on Russell and his teammates, however; it catapulted their confidence upward, and from that game on they felt they could compete against anyone they played. In the following game, Coach Woolpert replaced Bill Bush with Hal Perry in the starting lineup, which also included Russell, Jones, Jerry Mullen, and Stan Buchanan. The Dons proceeded to destroy a solid Oregon State team, 60–34. According to Jones, "The beauty of it was that Bill Bush said, 'That's well and good.' There was no hassle about him being demoted. He said, 'This is best for the team, and I'll do it coming off the bench.'"

The next test for the new lineup was the same UCLA squad that had defeated the Dons two games earlier. This time, the matchup was held in San Francisco instead of Los Angeles, and the change of venue served the Dons well: They romped to a 56–44 win. Next, the team traveled to Oklahoma City to play in the All-College Tournament. Their first game went like clockwork; they dispatched Wichita State with ease. The host team was USF's next opponent, and Oklahoma City fell 4 points short of the Dons' total of 75. In the tournament finals, USF easily defeated George Washington University. The remainder of the Dons' regular season was played primarily on the West Coast, where Russell's intimidating defense and scoring average of more than 20 points per game led USF to a sweep of its schedule.

The next stop for the team in 1955 was the NCAA championship tournament. They beat West Texas State in San Francisco, traveled to Corvalis, Oregon, to beat Utah, and then defeated Oregon State, 57–56, on their home floor. This narrow vic-

A fully extended Russell soars to the basket over all-American Willie Naulls (33) of the UCLA Bruins. The USF center later said that he practiced "jumping continually at the backboard until I could go up to the rim thirty-five times without stopping. If you build up your timing and your legs like that over the years you have an edge."

On a road trip with the Dons, Russell pauses to please some young fans by signing his autograph. Nearly a decade later, he resolved to stop giving out what he regarded as worthless pieces of paper with his name on it—a decision that did not gain the public's approval. "I don't work for acceptance," Russell explained in a 1964 Saturday Evening Post interview. "It doesn't make any difference whether the fans like me or not. To me or to them. If they like me and I put up a poor performance, I will still be booed."

tory won the Dons a trip to Kansas City, Missouri, and the chance to play in the Final Four for the first time in the school's history.

Russell scored 24 points in the NCAA tournament semifinals and snatched a bushel of rebounds as USF defeated the University of Colorado, 62–50, and claimed a spot in the finals. In their quest for a national championship, the Dons were matched against a powerful team from La Salle College. The Philadelphia-based school had an outstanding center in Tom Gola and was expected to thrash its cross-country rival.

Russell and Jones had a different outcome in mind. Russell scored 23 points and pulled down 25 rebounds, and Jones pitched in with 24 points. The Dons won the game handily, by a margin of 14 points. Claiming the national title provided a thrilling climax to a whirlwind season that saw USF win 25 games in a row. Russell, who averaged 21.4 points and 21.5 rebounds per game for the 1954–55 season, topped off the year by being named the NCAA tournament's most valuable player.

Buoyed by his recent string of successes, Russell began to think for the first time about becoming a professional basketball player. ❧

4

"JUST GET
THE BALL"

❦

DURING THE SUMMER of 1955, Bill Russell and his girlfriend, Rose Swisher, drove cross-country with his father and stepmother to attend a meeting at the White House. He had been invited to Washington, D.C., along with a number of other prominent sports figures, to appear at a luncheon hosted by President Dwight D. Eisenhower to promote physical fitness. During his summer break, Russell also joined his USF teammates on a U.S. State Department–sponsored goodwill tour of Latin America. Thanks to his abilities as a basketball player, Russell's horizons were already beginning to expand beyond his wildest dreams.

When Russell returned to USF for his senior year, he decided to go out for the school's track team. He proved to be an excellent high jumper, clearing the bar at a height of 6 feet 9¼ inches—just a few inches shy of a world record leap. But it soon became time for him to return to the business of playing basketball.

As the 1955–56 basketball season began that fall, Russell had to adjust to competing without the help of two key teammates, Jerry Mullen and Stan Buchanan, who had graduated the previous spring. Coach Phil Woolpert managed to ease their loss by recruiting three fine players: Carl Boldt, Mike Farmer, and Gene

Russell certainly had a lot to smile about in early 1956. In addition to receiving 2 trophies for his outstanding performance in the East-West College All-Star Game at New York City's Madison Square Garden, the all-American center saw his college team finish the season with both a perfect 29 and 0 record and a second straight national championship.

Brown. In addition, K. C. Jones was still with the team. Because appendicitis had caused him to miss almost all of the 1953–54 season, Jones was still eligibile to play intercollegiate sports at USF for another year—his fifth at the school—although he would not be allowed to play in the NCAA championships should the Dons qualify for the postseason tournament.

Russell also had to adjust on the court to a newly instituted collegiate rule. His dominating play near the basket had prompted the NCAA Rules Com-

In addition to playing basketball at USF, Russell was also a high jumper on the school's track team. His personal best was a near-world-record leap of 6 feet 9¼ inches.

mittee to widen the foul lane, in which an offensive player can remain for only 3 seconds, from 6 to 12 feet. The rule was intended to move the bigger players away from the basket, but it also caused the offense to spread out more and thus helped the better defensive clubs, such as USF.

The defending national champions faced their first real test early in the season, at New York's Madison Square Garden, where they took part in the Holiday Festival Tournament, which featured a stiff field of competition. The Dons began the Christmastime tournament by thumping the runners-up in the previous year's NCAA finals, La Salle, by 17 points. Russell owned the backboards, hauling down 22 rebounds, and added 26 points. In the tournament semifinals, he grabbed 22 rebounds and tallied 24 points as the Dons defeated a Holy Cross team that starred Tom Heinsohn.

Russell displayed more of the same kind of play in the finals. He netted 17 points and 18 rebounds as USF buried UCLA by 17. Now the entire country knew that the Russell-led Dons were one of the greatest college teams of all time.

A month later, in a game against the University of California at Berkeley, former Dons coach Pete Newell tried to slow the action down to a crawl, but his strategy failed as USF won the low-scoring contest, 33–24. It was the team's 40th straight victory. By the time the NCAA tournament began, the Dons had won 51 in a row. Their average margin of victory was 20 points per game, an increase of 5 over the previous season.

In spite of the Dons' perfect record, Russell grew worried as the team prepared for the national championships without Jones. "No man will miss K. C. during the tournament as much as I will," he said at the time. "You take a sling shot. I'm the forks and K. C. is the rubber band. He makes the operation go." But Woolpert inserted Gene Brown in Jones's spot, and the Dons hardly missed a beat. The team whisked by both UCLA and Utah and then whipped Southern Methodist University in the NCAA semifinals by 20 points. USF capped off its perfect season by hammering a talented Iowa team by 12 points, giving Russell and his school a second straight national championship. The Dons' streak of consecutive wins, which finally ended at 60, remained a record until Bill Walton led the UCLA Bruins to 88 straight wins during the early 1970s.

Russell was just as dominating in the 1955–56 campaign as he had been the previous year. For the second season in a row, he averaged more than 20 points and 20 rebounds per game. (The next collegiate player to perform such a feat in a *single* season was Kermit Washington of American University, and he did it nearly 20 years later.) Nevertheless, leading the Dons to a national championship was not as easy a task for Russell the second time around. Throughout the season, he had been thinking about the day when he would turn professional. "Whenever I walked on the court," he said, "I began to calculate how this particular game might affect my future. Thoughts of money and prestige crept into my head."

Even so, Russell had other business to take care of before he could join the professional ranks. One of his decisions involved school: Not wanting to slight his studies, he elected to reduce his course load rather than attempt to graduate in the spring of 1956 with the rest of his class. Playing basketball for USF cut into his classroom hours, and he realized that when spring rolled around he would be shy of graduating by about a semester's worth of credits. Rather than cut corners by taking easy courses to satisfy his graduation requirements, he resolved to complete his studies the following year, and he lived up to his promise.

Russell did not try to finish up at school that summer because he had his mind set on playing for the U.S. Olympic basketball team at the Summer Games, which were to begin that October in Melbourne, Australia. Abe Saperstein, founder of the Harlem Globetrotters, a troupe of talented black basketball players who incorporated slapstick comedy routines into their games, had something else in mind for Russell. Saperstein tried to entice Russell to join his traveling team.

The USF standout and his college coaches met with Saperstein in Chicago, but Russell turned down an offer to sign with the Globetrotters without any

Russell puts the finishing touches on the Dons' perfect season as he blocks a shot in the 1956 national collegiate finals against the Iowa Hawkeyes. A key to playing winning basketball, he said, was to "learn the other man's habits. Then make him go exactly opposite to what he likes to do."

Star of the 1956 U.S. Olympic basketball team, Russell shakes hands with towering Soviet Union center Ivan Krouminch following their first meeting in the round-robin tournament, held in Melbourne, Australia. After the U.S. cagers trounced the Soviets, 85–55, on November 29, Russell and his mates vanquished them again 2 days later, 89–55, to capture the gold medal.

second thoughts. He wanted to remain an amateur athlete for the next several months so he could qualify for the Olympic team. He also wanted to take a crack at playing in the NBA.

In mid-1956, Russell and Jones tried out for and made the Olympic team. They were joined by 10 other players—Richard Boushka, Carl Cain, Charles Darling, William Evans, Gilbert Ford, Burdette Haldorson, William Hougland, Robert Jeangerard, Ronald Tomsic, and James Walsh—none of whom went on to enjoy a professional career of much note. The team prepared for the Summer Games by playing a series of exhibition games around the country, then made a goodwill trip to South America on behalf of the State Department before journeying farther south to Australia and the Olympics.

Although most of Russell's Olympic basketball teammates were not of professional caliber, they were obviously talented, or else they would not have been invited to represent their country. Nevertheless, the team destroyed its competition in the Games by riding the backs of Russell and Jones. "It was one of the biggest thrills of my life," Russell said of his Olympic experience, in *Go Up for Glory*. The U.S. squad played 8 games and won all 8 by at least 30 points. Their average margin of victory on the way to winning the gold medal was an astounding 53 points.

On December 9, three days following his return to the United States from Australia, Russell had another reason to celebrate: He and Rose Swisher were married at the Taylor Methodist Church in Oakland. A week later, after a honeymoon in nearby Carmel, the young couple flew to Boston. It was time for Russell's professional career to begin.

The Boston Celtics had claimed Russell in basketball's annual draft of college seniors, thanks to

Russell and his bride, the former Rose Swisher, are congratulated by members of the 1956 U.S. Olympic basketball team following their wedding on December 9, just three days after Russell returned from the Olympic Games in Australia.

The beginning of a beautiful relationship: Russell confers with Red Auerbach on December 18, 1956, at Madison Square Garden, shortly before signing a contract to play with the Boston Celtics. Russell made his professional debut the following night against the Hawks in St. Louis.

Red Auerbach's shrewd maneuvering with the St. Louis Hawks. The Celtics coach and general manager, convinced that Russell possessed the right ingredients to make the Boston franchise a winner, had mortgaged a good portion of his team's talent for the right to sign the USF and Olympic star. The Celtics had traded all-star center Easy Ed Macauley along with Cliff Hagan, just out of the army and sure to be a quality forward, for St. Louis's first pick, the second selection in the entire draft. The Rochester Royals owned the first pick, but Auerbach had learned that they had no intention of choosing Russell.

When the Royals opted for Sihugo Green, the path was clear for Russell to become a Celtic. He signed right away with Boston for $19,500 and immediately joined the club, which had already opened up its season. "You're probably worried about scoring because everyone says you don't shoot well enough to play ball," Auerbach told him.

"Well, yes, I am a little concerned about that," Russell said.

"Okay, I'll make a deal with you today, right here and now," Auerbach responded. "I promise that as long as you play here, whenever we talk about contracts we will *never* discuss statistics. Russ, we have a pretty good organization here. No cliques; everyone gets along real well. All we want you to do is something no one's ever been able to do for this team: Get us the ball. Forget everything else. Just get the ball."

5

THE DYNASTY
BEGINS

Celtics owner Walter Brown welcomes to the Boston franchise his first-round pick in the 1956 college senior draft. An all-American performer and Olympic gold medalist, Russell wound up spending his entire playing career with the Celtics.

THE BOSTON CELTICS already held the best record in the league, 13 and 3, when Bill Russell joined them in December 1956. No other team in the NBA boasted as talented a starting unit or as deep a bench. Nor did any other club play the sport of basketball the way the Celtics did.

Boston's selfless approach to the game became apparent to Russell immediately after his first practice with his new teammates. Arnie Risen, the incumbent center, knew that Russell had been brought into the organization for the express purpose of taking his own starting job. Nevertheless, Risen took the 22-year-old Russell aside after the practice and showed him some of the tricks that centers around the league would try against the rookie. By tutoring Russell, Risen was hastening his own departure from the squad. Yet the veteran chose to help the ball club rather than worry about his future with the team. The Celtics players, Russell realized, were dedicated to working with one another.

Russell also learned early on that Red Auerbach was a man of his word; the Boston coach stood by his little speech about the defensive-minded center not having to score points. When a rumor spread throughout the league that Russell could not shoot

Early in his rookie season with the Celtics, Russell sought to convince the critics who said he was a poor shooter that they were wrong; he soon learned, however, that he was at his best when focusing on other aspects of the game. "In order to win," he said later, "you have to get yourself past a lot of things that may not be vital to winning but make you feel good, like scoring a lot of points."

very well, he tried to prove his critics wrong by taking shots from the outside, like the Syracuse Nationals' Dolph Schayes, the Philadelphia Warriors' Neil Johnston, and some of the NBA's other big men did. "What the hell are you doing shooting from way out there," Auerbach finally screamed at Russell, "besides making a fool of yourself?" From that moment on, Russell never again tried to prove he could score a lot of points in the NBA.

He didn't need to. The Celtics had plenty of other players who could put the ball in the basket, including another rookie, Tom Heinsohn. The scoring ability Heinsohn had displayed at Holy Cross translated nicely to the pro game, and he was one of the reasons for the team's fast start.

Joining Heinsohn on the starting five were Risen, the ball-handling wizard Bob Cousy, the sharpshooting Bill Sharman, and the burly Jim Loscutoff, nicknamed Jungle Jim because of his physical style of play. The first player to come off the bench was Frank Ramsey, who filled his role so admirably that having a game-breaking "sixth man" has become a Celtics tradition. Dick Hemric, Jack Nichols, and Andy Phillip were the other backups who helped make Boston a formidable presence in the league. And then there was Russell.

The Celtics at first took a step backward when Russell was added to the squad. The sense of cohesion the team had developed during its training camp and the early portion of the season suffered a bit upon his arrival. Not until Boston had played about a dozen games with Russell in the starting lineup did the team return to its early-season form.

By then, the Celtics had grown accustomed to having Russell as their man in the middle. He was an easy person to play with. He did not demand to have the ball in his hands, the way a number of other NBA players did; yet he retrieved the ball off the backboard with greater regularity than any other player in the league. Whenever a teammate slipped up and allowed his man to drive toward the basket, Russell was there to stop him.

What made Russell's defensive play all the more extraordinary was that when he went up to block a shot, he shunned swatting it into the stands. Today, most players like to reject a shot as emphatically as possible, which usually results in their smashing the ball out of bounds. Russell always tried to steer the ball in the direction of a teammate or toward a spot on the floor where he could gather it in, thereby giving his team an additional chance to score. As his skills developed, he also became adept at converting defensive rebounds into scoring chances by firing the ball downcourt to fast-breaking teammates. This technique became one of the Celtics' most devastating weapons: the ability to shut down the opposition at one end of the floor and then lay the ball in the hoop at the other end with almost contemptuous ease.

With Russell in the fold, the Celtics went on to register a 44 and 28 record, the best in the league. They were seeded first in the Eastern Division play-offs, earning them a bye in the division's semifinal round, which saw Syracuse play Philadelphia for the right to meet Boston in the Eastern Division finals. The Nationals dispatched the Warriors in two straight games, then began a best-of-five-games series with the Celtics. But Syracuse left the playoffs in a hurry, as Boston whipped them in three straight games.

The 1956–57 NBA finals, a best-of-seven-games series, matched the Celtics against the St. Louis Hawks, led by one of the league's top scorers, Bob Pettit. Having finished the regular season with a 34 and 38 record, the Hawks were prohibitive favorites to be trounced by Boston. But when the underdogs won the opener in double overtime, on the Celtics' home floor in Boston Garden, it became apparent that St. Louis was not intimidated by the excellent won-lost record posted throughout the year by Russell and his teammates.

The Celtics bounced back to win Game 2 by 20 points. But St. Louis again gained the upper hand by winning the third game, 106–98. Boston took the next two contests, giving them the opportunity to put away the Western Division champions, but the Hawks refused to succumb. They defeated the Celtics once again by two points, to set up a final, winner-take-all game in Boston Garden.

This decisive matchup, which took place on April 13, 1957, was one of the most dramatic—and one of the most important—games ever played in the NBA. According to *The NBA's Official Encyclopedia of Pro Basketball,*

Six times the Celtics seemed to take command; each time the Hawks caught up. In the closing seconds, two free throws by Pettit sent the game into overtime. In the closing seconds of the extra period, a basket by [Jack] Coleman forced another overtime. In the last two seconds of the second overtime, a free throw by Loscutoff increased Boston's lead to 125–123—and a last-second shot by Pettit, which could have meant another overtime, bounced off the rim.

A large television audience saw this game . . . and the visibility of the NBA took a quantum jump.

And Bill Russell, who had averaged 13.9 points and 24.4 rebounds per playoff game, was perhaps the

Ball-handling wizard Bob Cousy (14) passes the ball to the Celtics' high-scoring rookie, Tom Heinsohn (left), during the 1957 NBA finals against the St. Louis Hawks. One reason why Russell was free to concentrate on defense was that many of the other Boston players—including Cousy and Heinsohn, who were later voted into the Basketball Hall of Fame—possessed superior offensive skills.

Russell "in training" in the base-ment of his Reading, Massachu-setts, home in early 1958. One of the ways he escaped the rigors of professional basketball was by operating a model train collec-tion—a hobby that evoked the days during his boyhood in Louisi-ana when he sat along the rail-road tracks and watched the trains go by.

most visible player of all. Indeed, there was no one else like him in the world of basketball. Adding two national collegiate titles, an Olympic gold medal, and now an NBA championship to his credentials in a little more than a year, Russell stood alone in his sport. "A champion must forget greatness and must be simply the man that you have to beat at his best under pressure," he said in *Go Up for Glory*. At the age of 23, Russell had clearly demonstrated that he, as much as anyone, knew what it took to be a winner.

What was more, he wanted to remain a winner. "I decided that professional sports is about winning," Russell wrote in *Second Wind*, "and so I made up my mind that I wanted to win every game." Even though he was not able to reach that goal as a professional—after having nearly managed such a feat as a colle-gian—he devoted himself to this task and shunned personal honors, such as winning the scoring and rebounding titles and commanding the highest salary in the league. It soon became clear that Russell's supremely competitive attitude was virtually un-matched in the NBA, even by most of the other great players in the league.

Russell combined this attitude with a keen in-telligence that enabled him to understand just what it took to win a game. He knew which shots to at-tempt to block in a given game: only those that he thought would affect the final outcome. If he tried to block every shot he could put his hands on, he might encourage his opponents to shoot from farther out, thereby cutting into his ability to control the action. Instead, Russell tried to give the impression that he *might* block every shot, thus causing the shooter to look out for him instead of concentrating totally on the basket; but for the purpose of dictating play he usually went after only a dozen or so shots in each game.

Off the court, Russell enjoyed a banner day in late 1957. Less than 24 hours after he and his wife moved into their new home in Reading, Massachu-setts, Rose gave birth to Bill, Jr. The couple's first child was later joined by two siblings, Jacob and Karen.

Russell's second NBA campaign went by more smoothly than his initial year did, primarily because he attended training camp before the season began. All of the Celtics seemed to benefit from his first full year with the team, as the men in kelly green posted a league-leading 49 victories—8 more than the next-best total, accomplished by the Nationals and the Hawks. Russell averaged 16.6 points and an astound-ing 22.7 rebounds per game, improving on his first-year averages of 14.7 points and 19.6 rebounds. He also finished the 1957–58 season third in the league in field-goal percentage.

Instead of facing the second-place Nationals in the Eastern Division finals, the Celtics were matched against Paul Arizin and the upset-minded Warriors, who had surprised Syracuse in the first round of the

Russell and the Celtics appeared to be heading for their second straight league championship (above) as they squared off against the St. Louis Hawks in the 1958 NBA finals. But when the Boston center had to be helped off the floor in Game 4 (opposite page) after he severely injured his ankle, the Celtics wound up losing not only their best player but the series.

playoffs. But Philadelphia was not as fortunate against Boston. The Celtics defeated them in five games and advanced to the NBA finals for the second year in a row.

Waiting for Boston in the championship series were the St. Louis Hawks, eager to avenge their double-overtime loss in Game 7 the previous April. The first 3 games of the 1958 NBA finals mirrored the start of the 1957 championship series: The Hawks won close contests in Games 1 and 3 and took a 2–1 lead in the rematch.

The next meeting contained a moment that marked the turning point of the series: Russell severely sprained his ankle while going after a rebound and could not continue to play. His teammates rallied without him for a 109–98 victory and evened the series at 2 games apiece. But the drop-off in talent with Russell out of the lineup proved too much for Boston to overcome. St. Louis won Game 5 by a basket.

Russell tried to play in Game 6 with a plaster cast surrounding his ankle. It became apparent after a few minutes that this measure was not working, and he was removed from the game, only to watch the Celtics lose the series finale by a single point. Had a healthy Russell been on the court, Boston might very well have had a chance to celebrate its second straight championship.

The 1957–58 season ended on a doubly disappointing note for Russell. Although he was voted the league's most valuable player, the nation's sportswriters failed to name him to the all-NBA team. Instead of placing a center, two forwards, and two guards on the team, as had been the custom, the writers opted for three forwards and two guards rather than include Russell, the league's top center, on the squad.

Russell suspected that racial discrimination had a good deal to do with this shocking omission and suggested there was a quota throughout the league for blacks. Today, blacks comprise an overwhelming majority of the players in the NBA. But in 1958, no team carried more than three blacks on its roster. The owners wanted it that way, Russell said, and so did the fans.

That trend began to change during the next decade. And Russell, who spoke out against "latent anti–black man prejudice" in professional basketball, helped bring it about. "I don't want people to stereotype me ever," he said in 1958. "You know, they think that every time a colored man goes places, the first thing he does is get himself a Cadillac. I like a Cadillac. I drove 'em lots of times. But I wouldn't buy one—you couldn't give me one. I bought my Chrysler last year."

6

THE RUN OF
THE RINGS

As THE SUMMER of 1958 wore on, Bill Russell grew eager to begin his third year with the Boston Celtics; he wanted to erase the ugly memory of the past season, which marked the first time in four years his team did not win a championship. But he would do more than capture another title. Beginning with the 1958–59 NBA season, he and the Celtics would enjoy a spree that proved to be the greatest run of championships in all of professional sports.

A key to Boston's unrivaled success was the addition of K. C. Jones to the squad. After twice failing to make the team, Russell's college roommate finally won a spot on the Celtics roster. When he wound up his playing career nine years later, he had been instrumental in eight straight NBA titles and had earned himself a place in the Basketball Hall of Fame.

During that eight-year stretch, many extraordinary basketball players entered the professional ranks. But none of them could manage to wrest the league crown from the Celtics. In 1958–59, the newest star to shine in the NBA was Elgin Baylor, the pride of Washington, D.C., and Seattle University. The moment he stepped on the floor for the Minneapolis Lakers, a new dimension was introduced to the sport of pro basketball: the act of soaring into the air with

Russell guards Philadelphia Warriors rookie Wilt Chamberlain during the 1960 Eastern Division finals. A golden era in professional basketball, the late 1950s and early 1960s saw a number of gifted players—including Chamberlain, Elgin Baylor, Oscar Robertson, and Jerry West—establish themselves as stars in the NBA.

Elgin Baylor (22), whom Russell called "power personified," brought a new wrinkle to the pro game when he joined the Minneapolis Lakers in 1958: the act of soaring into the air with the ball and remaining there until the defense fell back and allowed a clear shot. The high-scoring forward's great leaping ability and exceptional body control helped transform the sport into a faster paced and more athletic type of contest.

the ball and remaining there, seemingly suspended above the court, until the defender fell back and allowed an uncontested shot.

Professional basketball was still in its formative stage during the 1950s. Body control was not an important part of the game; guards, forwards, and centers alike drove in a straight line to the basket and played at a deliberate pace. Baylor's great leaping ability began to change all that by helping to create a more athletic type of contest.

Russell had long since discovered he was an excellent jumper, and he and his teammates felt comfortable with this change in the game, for the Celtics were singly and collectively as physically gifted as any team in the league. Russell insists to this day that Tom Heinsohn was the most talented forward he ever saw. Bob Cousy was a whippet on the floor and a magician with the ball. Bill Sharman possessed the purest shooting eye this side of a more recent Celtics great, Larry Bird. Sixth man Frank Ramsey was, in the words of Coach Red Auerbach, "the most versatile player" around. And now there was also the hardworking, speedy Sam Jones, an expert bank shooter and the best clutch scorer on the team; he had joined Boston the previous year. With the addition of K. C. Jones and the bull-like Gene Conley (who spent the other half of the year pitching in the major leagues), the 1958 Celtics could run and jump with anyone.

But it all started and ended in the middle, with Russell. Able to dictate the action, he orchestrated victory after victory as Boston rolled to a league-high 52 and 20 record. Unlike the past two years, however, the Celtics did not face the St. Louis Hawks in the championship series. The Lakers, led by the 6-foot-5-inch Baylor, had darted past the Hawks in the Western Division finals.

The Celtics had nearly failed to reclaim their division title as well. Their opponents in the Eastern Division finals, the Syracuse Nationals, had acquired George Yardley, the previous year's scoring champion, to mesh his skills with those of center Dolph Schayes, forward Johnny Kerr, and two excellent guards, Hal Greer, a deadly marksman, and Larry Costello, a solid playmaker. This lineup almost did the Celtics in. The series seesawed back and forth; Boston and Syracuse, like two prizefighters who have been trading powerful blows, staggered into Boston Garden on April 1 for the seventh and deciding game of the deadlocked series. The Celtics came away with a hard-earned victory, 130–125.

The 1959 NBA championship series was, in comparison, something of an anticlimax. Heading into the series, the Celtics owned an 18-game winning streak against the Lakers. The last time the 2 teams had met, Boston had scored an amazing 173 points, the most ever tallied by an NBA team in a non-overtime game. So it came as no surprise when the Celtics trounced Minneapolis in four straight games and reclaimed the title of league champion.

Now a national figure, Russell accepted an invitation during the off-season to travel to Africa on behalf of the U.S. State Department. His journey took him to a number of nations, including Ethiopia, Ivory Coast, Sudan, and Liberia, where he wound up investing in a rubber plantation. He visited schoolrooms and held basketball clinics in several of the larger cities and toured villages scattered across the exotic landscape. In many of these hamlets, the villagers had never seen a black American before, let alone a 6-foot-10-inch basketball player.

Russell delighted in demonstrating some of the basic skills needed to play the sport. He taught the local children how to dribble a ball and how to shoot, forming his arms into a circle to turn himself into a makeshift basket for them. The joy he brought to these youngsters, who jumped and laughed and ran with him, indicated that Russell made an ideal ambassador of goodwill. By the time he returned to the United States, his love for playing sports was thoroughly replenished.

Playing for an owner such as Walter Brown and being coached by Red Auerbach helped to make the game all the more enjoyable. Russell deeply admired Brown. According to the star center, the Celtics owner "was goodness rewarded." When Abe Saperstein threatened Brown by telling him the Harlem Globetrotters would never grace Boston Garden if the Celtics broke the Globetrotters' stronghold on black talent by drafting a black player, Brown threw Saperstein out of his office and never again allowed the popular Globetrotters to set foot in the arena. Willing to take a financial beating to stick to his

principles, Brown was someone whom Russell looked up to with great respect.

Russell also held Auerbach, the mastermind behind Boston's rise to the top of the NBA, in high regard. Before Auerbach joined the Celtics in 1950, the team usually finished in the lower half of the standings. A tough taskmaster from New York City's Lower East Side, he quickly turned the franchise around. "I found players who wanted to win," he explained. "They didn't have what we like to call 'Celtic pride' or tradition when they got here. They acquired it. It rubbed off on them."

Auerbach's shrewd maneuvers consistently enhanced the team. He managed to draft ballplayers other general managers overlooked and made them fit smoothly into Boston's system. He did not need to rely on being one of the game's greatest court strategists, for he was a master psychologist who knew how to manipulate the ego of each player to get the most out of his performance. "If you were to rate the

Russell positions himself to help out the hardworking Sam Jones as the Boston backcourtman fights through a screen while covering the Cincinnati Royals' Oscar Robertson. Jones teamed up with Bob Cousy and K. C. Jones to give the Celtics a trio of talented guards in the late 1950s and early 1960s.

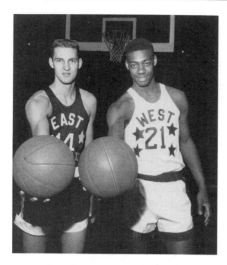

Excelling in every phase of the game, Jerry West (left) and Oscar Robertson (right) entered the league in 1960, joining, respectively, the Los Angeles Lakers and Cincinnati Royals. Their all-around play later prompted Russell to call them the top two guards in NBA history.

greatest coaches in the history of sports," Russell said of Auerbach, "his name must top the list."

The Celtics general manager and head coach was not the only member of the organization who got Russell to play his best night in and night out. K. C. Jones and Sam Jones irritated, taunted, and teased the rangy center to play harder on days when he felt fatigued. The equally good-natured Satch Sanders, who joined Boston in 1960, also helped keep Russell loose. And when John Havlicek came to the ball club in 1962, his tireless work habits and ability to concentrate inspired his teammates to perform at a similarly high level.

The Celtics needed to play hard, because as the defending NBA champs they were being hunted by every other team in the league. This pursuit reached even greater dimensions during the 1959–60 season, when Wilt Chamberlain entered the circuit. The 7-foot-1-inch, 275-pound "Goliath" (as Chamberlain occasionally referred to himself) became Russell's greatest nemesis in the NBA.

Having led the University of Kansas to the NCAA finals in 1957, Chamberlain left school after his junior year to join the Harlem Globetrotters. He subsequently signed with the Philadelphia Warriors, causing the balance of power to tilt a bit toward his new team, for he was every bit as dominating in the pros as he had been in college.

Warriors owner Eddie Gottlieb made sure that Chamberlain would be Philadelphia's center of attention. Gottlieb, who believed that a crowd paid its money to watch a ballplayer score rather than play defense, insisted on having his team funnel the ball to the Big Dipper. Chamberlain averaged 37.6 points per game during his rookie season—the most ever by an NBA player—and outrebounded everyone, even Russell.

In spite of Chamberlain's dominating play, the Warriors finished the regular season 10 games behind the Celtics, who ended the campaign with a 59 and 16 mark. Philadelphia got past Syracuse in the first round of the playoffs but was whipped by Boston in the Eastern Division finals. By negating Chamberlain's outstanding individual effort, the triumphant Celtics demonstrated that professional basketball was still a team sport and not a one-man show.

This time around, the St. Louis Hawks kept their appointment with the Celtics in the NBA finals. Led once again by Bob Pettit, the Hawks slogged past the Lakers in seven games for the right to face Boston for the third time in four years. Beginning on March 27, the top two teams in the NBA traded games back and forth, until the series came down to one final contest to decide the championship. The Celtics waltzed to a 122–103 victory in Game 7.

The 1960–61 season saw guards Oscar Robertson and Jerry West enter the league through the college draft. Both players exhibited awesome talent; Russell later called them the two best guards in NBA history. The Big O, as Oscar Robertson was known, led the league in assists and finished third in scoring during his rookie year; yet his team, the Cincinnati Royals, finished in last place in the Western Division. West, an all-around player who averaged 17.6 points during his initial campaign, soon earned the nickname Mr. Clutch because of his uncanny ability to score the big basket with the game on the line. He suited up for the Los Angeles Lakers, the franchise having just moved to the West Coast from Minneapolis.

Once again, the Celtics won the Eastern Division (with a 57 and 22 record), and the Hawks finished first in the West. Like old friends, the two teams met in the NBA finals. This time, it took Boston just five games to win the league title. Russell averaged nearly 30 rebounds a game during the postseason and won his second Most Valuable Player Award.

Whereas Russell was revolutionizing the way people played defense, Chamberlain was going wild in

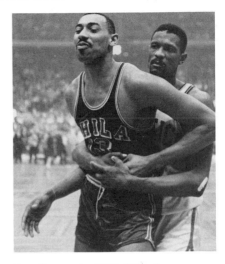

Russell restrains Wilt Chamberlain during a heated moment in the 1962 Eastern Division finals. "Chamberlain and I carried on a friendship the entire time we played basketball together," Russell said, "even though the newspapers portrayed us as mortal enemies."

NBA commissioner Maurice Po-
doloff (right) presents Russell with
the Most Valuable Player Award
for his play during the 1961–62
season. The Boston center won
the award five times in his career.

the scoring department. In the 1961–62 season, after leading the league in scoring two years in a row, the Philadelphia pivotman outdid even himself. Against the New York Knickerbockers on March 2, 1962, the Warriors center made 36 of 63 field goals and connected on 28 of 32 free throws to score a record 100 points in one game. He overpowered the rest of the league as well, averaging 50.4 points per game for the season (nearly 20 points per game more than the next-highest scorer, Walt Bellamy of the Chicago Packers, a newly formed expansion team).

The Celtics preserved their dynasty by a very slim margin in 1962, and it was Chamberlain who led the siege. Despite setting a franchise record with 60 wins during the regular season, Boston barely edged past Philadelphia in the Eastern Division finals. With the series knotted up at 3 games apiece, it took a jump shot by Sam Jones with 2 seconds left on the clock to give the Celtics a 109–107 win in Game 7 and end Chamberlain's magic season.

Eleven days later, the Lakers found themselves in an excellent position to overthrow the defending champions. They led the series, three games to two. All Baylor, West, and company had to do was take Game 6 on their home court or win the game after that. But Los Angeles was unable to pull off the upset. The Celtics held fast in Game 6, 119–105, and the series returned to Boston Garden for a final showdown.

With a second remaining in the fourth quarter of Game 7 and the score tied, Frank Selvy of the Lakers took a shot that rolled along the rim before it fell to the Garden's parquet floor at the buzzer. If the ball had gone in the basket, Los Angeles would have captured the championship. Instead, the ball game went into overtime, and the Celtics won it in the extra session, 110–107, to earn a fourth straight NBA title. Russell was again voted the league's most valuable player, in spite of Chamberlain's amazing scoring feats.

The 1962–63 season offered more of the same: Russell won his fourth Most Valuable Player Award as the Celtics again wore the league crown. This time, Boston beat Oscar Robertson and the Cincinnati Royals in the Eastern Division finals and then routed the Lakers in the championship series. As far as Russell was concerned, there was a new wrinkle to this, his seventh season in the NBA. For the first time since Chamberlain had entered the league, Russell was voted by the nation's sportswriters and broadcasters to the all-NBA team, even though Chamberlain had averaged 44.8 points per game—28 points above Russell's average. It had become clear to almost everyone—just as it had to Russell, Auerbach, and the Celtics—that defense won basketball games. ✺

7

THE MAN IN
THE MIDDLE

THREE MONTHS AFTER the 1962–63 season ended, Bill Russell received a phone call from Charles Evers, the brother of slain civil rights leader Medgar Evers, whom white racists had gunned down outside his Jackson, Mississippi, home one month earlier. Charles Evers thought the 29-year-old Russell could help calm the tension-wracked city by holding a series of basketball clinics for black and white youths.

Russell was not eager to journey to Mississippi: His large frame would make an enormous target for any bigot who might want to take a shot at him. His Celtics teammates tried to lighten the situation by advising him to keep a low profile.

Previous events in 1963 had given Russell a reason to fear making a public appearance in the Deep South. That April, the Reverend Martin Luther King, Jr., the nation's acknowledged leader in the fight for racial justice, began staging nonviolent protests in another southern city, Birmingham, Alabama, as part of his campaign to force public facilities to become desegregated. The Birmingham police responded to these demonstrations by unleashing attack dogs and high-pressure water hoses on the marchers, many of whom were children.

Russell and Boston Red Sox pitcher Earl Wilson attend a memorial service for slain civil rights leader Medgar Evers in June 1963. Russell, who played an active role in the fight for racial equality, maintained, "There can be no neutrals in the battle for human rights."

More violence occurred nine days later, on a Saturday evening in May. First, the home of King's brother, a Birmingham preacher, was firebombed. Minutes later, another bomb exploded outside King's Birmingham headquarters, triggering a riot in the city's streets.

President John F. Kennedy responded to the turmoil the following month. Saying he wanted "this nation to fulfill its promise" of freedom for all, the president proposed legislation to bar segregation in public accommodations and schools. In reaction to this proposal, Medgar Evers was assassinated by white racists a few hours later.

Even though Russell felt as though he would be walking into a lion's den, he decided to go to Jackson. Like Mister Charlie and the Old Man, who used to say, "Noviolent is what I am before someone hits me," he refused to kowtow to anybody. Later that summer, he also took part in the March on Washington for Jobs and Freedom, a massive civil rights demonstration held in the nation's capital.

Occasionally, Russell's insistence on marching his own way got him into trouble with the public. When he finally tired of being besieged with requests for his autograph and decided to stop giving out his signature, people began to label him an ingrate and a troublemaker for not acting the way a sports hero should. At one point, he tried to reach a compromise by mailing a small poster of himself to some of the autograph seekers. Nevertheless, he was still accused of ignoring one of the basic rights of all sports fans.

But Russell did not play professional sports because he wanted to be fawned over and treated as a celebrity. He donned the Celtics' green and white night after night chiefly because he loved to play basketball. He always gave his best effort whenever he stepped onto the court. There was no need, he felt, for anything more to be asked of him.

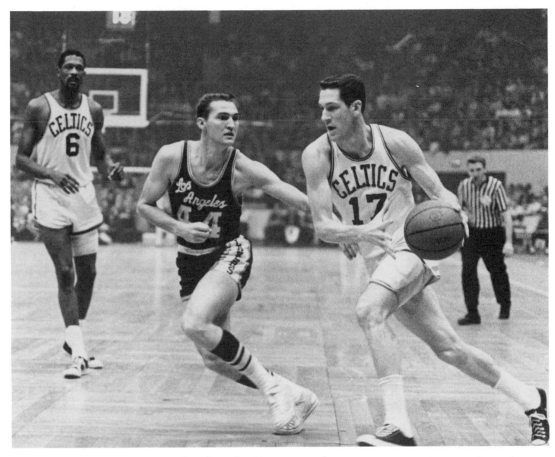

The 1963–64 season, the first for Boston without its backcourt wizard Bob Cousy, gave further proof that Russell put everything he had into the game. Many people regarded Cousy as the cornerstone of the franchise. They soon discovered otherwise.

The Celtics remained loaded at the guard spot, thanks to the Jones Boys, K. C. and Sam. Moreover, Boston had five good forwards—the starters Sanders and Heinsohn, plus Havlicek, the versatile Frank Ramsey, and Jim Loscutoff. Most important, they had the man in the middle, Russell, whom Auerbach named as cocaptain along with Ramsey. With this nucleus of players, the league's winningest team again captured the Eastern Division flag.

Russell looks on as Boston's perennial all-star, "sixth man" John Havlicek, drives past the Los Angeles Lakers' Jerry West. Russell said of the unselfish Havlicek, "If I were playing in an imaginary pick-up game among all the players I've ever seen, he's the first one I would choose for my side."

The Warriors, who had moved to San Francisco the previous season, won the Western Division title. They did it on the strength of the strategy devised by their new head coach, Alex Hannum, the same man who had guided St. Louis over Boston in the 1958 finals. Hannum had decided that the Celtics, having netted five titles in a row, understood how to play the game—defense won championships. So he made his Warriors concentrate on playing like the NBA titleholders, with Chamberlain imitating Russell's role on the Celtics. Chamberlain received a lot of support in guarding his own basket from a rookie, the enormously strong Nate Thurmond, who excelled at rebounding and playing defense.

In the 1964 playoffs, Boston dismissed Cincinnati in just five games, despite the addition to the Royals squad of a new star, rookie center Jerry Lucas, whose playing style complemented Oscar Robertson's brilliance. Then the Celtics did the same to the Warriors, needing just five games to claim their sixth straight NBA title. According to Russell, the team was getting better than ever because it was now playing tougher defense. The 1963–64 season was also sweet for him because he managed to play well despite suffering from arthritis in his knees.

The next season saw the renewal of the Boston-Philadelphia, Russell-Chamberlain rivalry, for the Warriors traded Chamberlain midway through the year, receiving $150,000 and 3 players from the Philadelphia 76ers, who had previously been the Syracuse Nationals (they had moved to Philadelphia the season before). The 76ers, with a record of 22 and 23 at the time of the trade, spent the rest of the schedule getting accustomed to their new center. Philadelphia wound up the season with a 40 and 40 record, far behind Boston's pace-setting 62 and 18 mark.

The Celtics had dedicated their pursuit of a seventh consecutive championship to the memory of

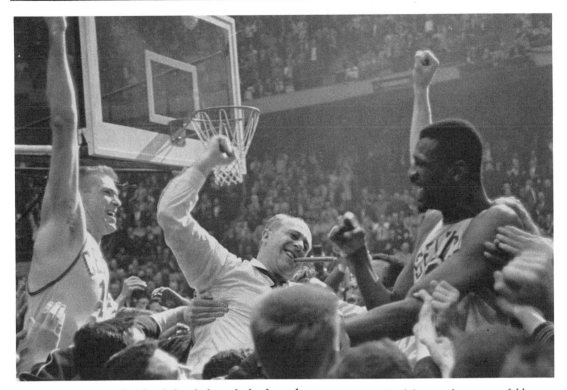

Walter Brown, who had died shortly before the season began. But during the postseason, Boston ran into a roadblock named Wilt Chamberlain, whose 76ers had beaten the Royals in the first round of the playoffs. Philadelphia was like a hungry lion that had been hiding in the tall grass; the 76ers were a much better team than their .500 record indicated. In fact, with Chamberlain now familiar with his new club's style of play, they were ready to challenge Boston for the Eastern Division title.

The two teams began the division finals on April 4, 1965, and six games later the series stood tied at three games apiece, with the seventh and deciding contest scheduled for April 15 at Boston Garden. With 2 minutes left in Game 7, the Celtics appeared to have a comfortable lead, 110–103. But as the clock wound down, Chamberlain scored the next six points, cutting the margin to one. Still, Boston

A jubilant mob scene unfolds on April 27, 1964, in Boston Garden as ecstatic Celtics fans carry Tom Heinsohn (left), Red Auerbach (center), and Russell around the court in celebration of the team's sixth consecutive NBA championship. "Success rode easily with the Celtics," Russell said. "I do not believe we ever became swell-headed. God knows, we had to fight for everything."

seemed to be in a commanding position: They were about to take possession of the ball with the lead and just three seconds remaining.

Then Russell made what was nearly the costliest mistake of his career. Inbounding the ball underneath the 76ers basket, he threw a pass that hit the guy wire supporting the backboard, thus turning the ball over to Philadelphia. "I just slammed my fist into the court and said: 'Oh my God . . . oh, my God . . . it's their ball,'" Russell remembered. Meanwhile, the 76ers called a time-out to set up their final attempt. If Chamberlain or one of his teammates could sink a shot, Boston's incredible run of championships would come to an end.

To make matters worse for the Celtics, they could not get out of their mind the memory of having blown Game 6 down the stretch 2 days earlier. It seemed as though their time to miss out on the NBA finals had arrived at last.

When play resumed, Hal Greer set himself to inbound the ball to Chet Walker, who was to dish it off to Chamberlain for the last shot. The actual sequence of events that took place, however, produced what turned out to be Celtics radio announcer Johnny Most's most famous call: "Havlicek stole the ball! Havlicek stole the ball!" In a flash, John Havlicek had streaked over from the foul line to intercept the pass and preserve Boston's victory—and their dynasty, as it turned out, for the Celtics dispatched the Lakers in five games to earn their seventh title in a row.

Prior to the start of the 1965–1966 season, Chamberlain became the first player in NBA history to receive an annual salary of $100,000. Shortly thereafter, the Boston front office made Russell the league's highest-paid player, in recognition of his ability to "just get the ball." He signed a 3-year contract for $100,001 per season, a hefty amount in the 1960s.

Being rewarded so handsomely did little to change Russell's approach to the sport. In the past, he would get so uptight before a game that he would have to vomit to release his nervous tension. "I don't get up as high for games now as I used to get," Russell said in late 1965. "Now I just throw up for playoffs."

The Celtics front office made some more news when Red Auerbach announced that the upcoming season would be his last one on the bench. He would continue as the team's general manager, however, and would appoint his successor as head coach in due time.

Intent on giving Auerbach an NBA title as a retirement present, the Celtics played solid ball all year and posted a sparkling 54 and 26 record. Nevertheless, Russell's 10th year with the team marked the first time in as many years that Boston did not win

"On the Celtics," Russell said, "we believed that the principal difference between good teams and great ones was mental toughness: how well a team could keep its collective wits under pressure." Led by the highly competitive Red Auerbach, Boston still experienced its share of heated moments, such as when Russell had to pull an angry Auerbach away from referee Sid Borgia.

Russell poses in 1964 with his three children: (from left to right) Jacob, Karen Kenyatta, and William, Jr.

the Eastern Division title. The 76ers finished the regular schedule one game up in the standings.

By failing to wind up in first place, Boston had to fight it out with Cincinnati for the right to take on Philadelphia, the new Eastern Division champs, in the division finals. When the Celtics fell behind against the Royals, two games to one, they found themselves needing two straight wins to advance into the next round of the playoffs. "You get this one, Russ," Sam Jones said to the Boston center before Game 4, "and you won't have to worry about the one back in Boston. I'll take care of that myself." Jones's comment let Russell know that the Celtics were still committed to winning the title for Auerbach.

With characteristic precision, Boston toppled the Royals and then the 76ers, making their way yet again to the NBA finals and another meeting with the Lakers. But Los Angeles was ready for the Celtics and took Game 1 in overtime, 133–129. Then Auerbach the master psychologist went to work. He decided the time had arrived to announce that Bill Russell would replace him as the team's coach.

The Boston players responded by rallying around Russell and grabbed the next three games. The Lakers refused to lie down, however; they pulled out the next two meetings. But the Celtics were not to be denied. They beat Los Angeles in Game 7, 95–93, in what was not really that close a contest.

Boston's incredible achievement of winning eight straight NBA championships was testimony to how closely knit and well constructed the Celtics were as a ball club and an organization. In fact, during Russell's 13 years as a player with the Celtics, Auerbach made only 1 trade: He sent backup center Mel Counts to Los Angeles for forward Bailey Howell in 1966. When a ballplayer began his career in Boston, he most likely ended it there.

As for Russell himself, he seemed to be more than just a Celtics player for life. With the start of the

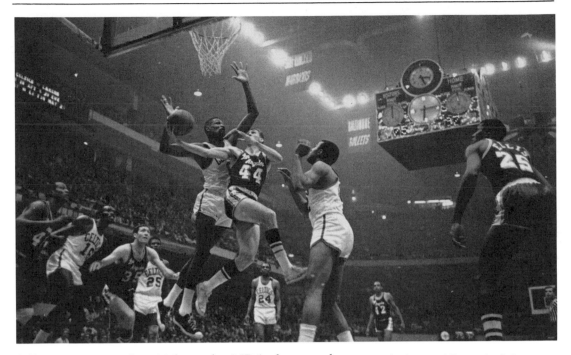

following season, his 11th in the NBA, he was about to become the nation's first black head coach of a major professional team. He did not know how the public would respond to his taking over the helm. But Russell understood that if he were to fail, people across the country would nod their head knowingly and say, "You see, they can play, but they can't think and coach." He had a lot to prove all over again. ❧

The heart of Boston's defense, Russell blankets Jerry West as the Los Angeles guard attempts a lay-up in the opening game of the 1965 NBA finals, held at Boston Garden. During Russell's 13 years with the team, the Celtics and the Lakers battled for the league title 7 times.

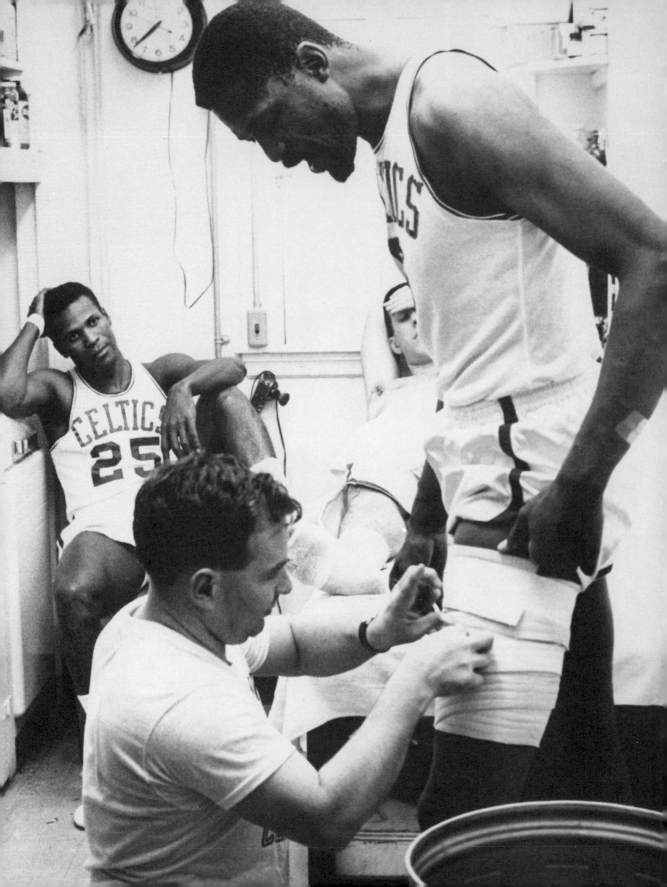

8

LETTING GO

❧

Russell has Celtics trainer Buddy LeRoux tape his thigh before a game as K. C. Jones looks on. "With the Celtics," Russell said, "I tried to play so that at the end of each season basketball and I would be even. Nobody would owe anybody anything."

BILL RUSSELL GUIDED the Boston Celtics to 60 wins during the 1966–67 season, his first as the team's head coach. He prepared himself for the job in much the same way that he had improved his play: by observing how others did it. He borrowed a page from Red Auerbach's book and learned to treat each player as an individual; some of the players needed to be encouraged, whereas others had to be badgered to give a better effort. (Russell, in fact, proved to be more of a disciplinarian than Auerbach was.) Russell also emulated his former coach in the way he ran the Celtics' practices.

Running the team during a game, however, was a much more difficult task for Russell than it had ever been for Auerbach. When Russell was on the court, he had to concentrate on rebounding, scoring, passing, and shutting down his man on defense, as he always did. But now he also had to be aware of many other details, including the job his teammates were doing. To compete in a game while evaluating the performance of his players proved to be quite a strain, although Boston's glowing regular-season record gave little indication that he had experienced difficulty in handling these extra demands.

Despite piling up 60 victories, the Celtics again finished second in the Eastern Division, for Wilt Chamberlain and the Philadelphia 76ers enjoyed a mammoth season, posting 68 wins against a mere 13 losses. Whereas Russell had spent the entire 1966–67 season learning how to combine playing with coaching, Chamberlain had spent the year discovering he did not have to be a one-man gang; the 76ers, with second-year-man Billy Cunningham, Hal Greer, Luke Jackson, Wali Jones, and others, boasted a championship-caliber squad. The Big Dipper halved the number of shots he had taken the previous year but saw his scoring average dip only 9 points, to a still-healthy 24.1 points per game. He finished third in the league in assists and his usual first in rebounds.

In the postseason, Boston swept by the New York Knickerbockers in the divisional semifinals, setting up a rematch of the past year's division finals. This time, it was the Celtics' turn to observe the art of team play. The 76ers smashed the reigning NBA champions, four games to one, in the Eastern Division finals and then polished off the San Francisco Warriors in six games for the league crown.

That summer, the 33-year-old Russell heard people murmur that he was getting kind of old. Indeed, the game was getting harder for him. His body was not nearly as lithe as it once was. The arthritis in his knees continued to be especially bothersome.

Nor was he finding life any easier off the court. As always, Russell continued to fight racial prejudice wherever he found it. This ordeal, while hard on him, helped inspire other black Americans to stand up for their civil rights. "I'm not a crusader who wants to stomp out evil everywhere," Russell wrote in *Second Wind*. "But I do take it as a duty to defend the freedoms that exist within our society, especially my own."

Self-defense proved to be necessary even in Boston, a city historically identified with the causes of freedom and racial justice. In Russell's opinion, the city's reputation was more a matter of legend than present-day reality; he often told reporters that he encountered more racism in Boston than he had in the South.

Apparently, there were people in Boston who never accepted Russell as a human being, despite his heroics on the court, and his readiness to speak his mind clearly enraged them. Russell's daughter, Karen, writing in the *New York Times Magazine* in 1987, recalled some ugly incidents from her childhood:

> One night we came home from a three-day weekend and found we had been robbed. Our house was in a shambles, and "NIGGA" was spray-painted on the walls. The burglars had poured beer on the pool table and ripped up the felt. They had broken into my father's trophy case and smashed most of the trophies. . . . Every time the Celtics went out on the road, vandals would come and tip over our garbage cans. My father went to the police station to complain. The police told him that raccoons were responsible, so he asked where he could apply for a gun permit. The raccoons never came back.

Russell's first day on the job as head coach of the Celtics. Red Auerbach's handpicked replacement leads Sam Jones (24), John Havlicek (17), and the other Boston players through a workout as they prepare for the 1966–67 season.

In the 1967 Eastern Division finals, Wilt Chamberlain (beneath basket) and the Philadelphia 76ers put a stop to K. C. Jones (25) and the Celtics' string of eight straight NBA titles. "I never thought we'd lose a single play-off series," Russell said, "except in 1967, when I knew Wilt's Philadelphia 76ers were a superior team."

Russell also worked hard to defend his reputation in the world of professional basketball, and in his second year as a head coach, his hard work paid off. During the 1967–68 regular season, Philadelphia again beat out Boston for the top spot in the Eastern Division. But when the two teams met in the division finals, Russell and his charges took their revenge. They beat the 76ers in seven games, then reclaimed the NBA championship by defeating the Los Angeles Lakers.

Russell's 12th year in the league was memorable for another reason: When the Celtics appeared in an exhibition game against the St. Louis Hawks in Alexandria, Louisiana, his paternal grandfather sat in the stands, watching his very first professional contest. Russell's father explained the rudiments of the game to the Old Man, but it was another aspect of the court action that intrigued the lifelong Louisianian even more. Near the end of the ball game, he asked Mister Charlie, "Do them white boys really have to do what William tells them to do?"

When the Old Man visited the Celtics player-coach in the locker room after the game, he received an even bigger shock: He spied Sam Jones, who was black, and one of his white teammates, John Havlicek, chatting jovially as they showered. "I never thought I'd live to see the day when the water would run off a white man onto a black man, and the water would run off a black man onto a white man," said an astonished Old Man Russell.

The times were indeed changing, and for Russell they were changing in more ways than one. The 1968–69 regular season did not go well at all for him and the Celtics. The NBA champions finished fourth in their division, behind the surprising Baltimore Bullets, the revamped 76ers, and the Knicks, led by Bill Bradley, Walt Frazier, and Willis Reed.

Part of the reason for this weak showing stemmed from Russell's inability to focus his entire attention on the court. The many road trips that had taken him away from his wife had helped create a gap in their relationship, and in 1969 he and Rose formally separated. That same year, he experienced a different kind of loss when the Old Man died.

Realizing that he was not playing at his usual high level, Russell decided midway through the 1968–69 season that the time had come for him to retire as a player. "A lot of it was that I just couldn't keep up," he said. It frustrated him to be unable to "let go" on the court.

Near the end of the regular season, in a game against the Bullets in the Baltimore Civic Center, the Celtics tied the score with just a few seconds remaining. In typical Boston fashion, they stole the ball and called a time-out, setting up an opportunity for a last-second, come-from-behind victory. As the arena vibrated from the howls and screams of thousands of fans, Russell called his teammates into a huddle to plan the last shot, then gazed at the faces of his fellow Celtics, each man's brow dripping with sweat.

"Now we've got 'em!" Russell yelled at his charges. "Let's go out there and kill 'em!" The players stood silently, waiting for their coach to outline his strategy. But all Russell did was laugh out loud—his characteristic, near-maniacal cackle. The thought had suddenly dawned on him that here he was, a giant of a man wearing gym clothes in front of an arena-sized crowd, yelling at his teammates to "kill 'em!"

"Coach," Bailey Howell finally asked, "what's the matter?"

Although Russell did not say it then, that moment on the Civic Center floor confirmed for him that the time had indeed come to retire: He was no longer approaching the game with his customary single-mindedness.

The rest of the year was clearly a struggle for the Celtics. Ever since Russell had joined the team, they had never finished the regular season lower than second place. For Russell, making his way through his 13th NBA campaign must have felt like running in wet sand. His scoring average dropped to the lowest mark of his professional career, 9.9 points per game. And while he still snared an average of 19.3 rebounds per game, Nate Thurmond had surpassed him as the league's second-leading rebounder (after Chamberlain, who had been traded to the Lakers after the 1967–68 season).

Then the playoffs began, and the NBA's second season seemed to give Russell and his teammates a second wind. The Celtics in the spring of 1969 were anything but a young team. Russell was 35 years old; Sam Jones was nearly 36; Bailey Howell was 32; and Satch Sanders was 30, as was Emmette Bryant. Yet

Player-coach Russell holds court with Tom "Satch" Sanders (16), Sam Jones (24), and John Havlicek (17). According to Russell, "Star players have an enormous responsibility beyond their statistics—the responsibility to pick their team up and carry it. You have to do this to win championships—and to be ready to do it when you'd rather be a thousand other places."

Russell's last stand: Making his final appearance in a Boston uniform, the Celtics player-coach battles Wilt Chamberlain and the Los Angeles Lakers in the 1969 NBA finals. Boston won the championship series in 7 games, giving Russell and the Celtics an unsurpassed record of 11 league titles in 13 years.

they had enough drive left to make one more dash through the playoffs. Boston's "old men" went up against Philadelphia in the Eastern Division semifinals and shook the life out of the 76ers' season. Then the Celtics defeated a strong Knicks team in six games. For the sixth time in the last eight years, Boston prepared to square off against Los Angeles for the NBA title.

With the addition of Chamberlain to an already impressive cast that included Elgin Baylor and Jerry

West, the Lakers looked like a sure bet to win the championship. Los Angeles took the first two games of the series, but Boston won the following game and evened things up when Sam Jones nailed a last-second bank shot in Game 4. The Lakers won the next game handily, but they failed to wrap up the series 2 days later in Boston; the Celtics' 99–90 victory set up yet another decisive seventh game, to be held in Los Angeles. It was to be Russell's last professional appearance as a player.

Russell reveled in the thought that his final game would pit him against his greatest adversary, Wilt Chamberlain, and in a winner-take-all scenario. The grand climax never arrived, however. The Celtics opened up a sizable lead in the fourth quarter and were never headed.

At the age of 35, Bill Russell left the NBA the same way he had entered it: as a champion. ☙

9

"AND WE'D ALL
LEVITATE"

BILL RUSSELL'S WORLD changed dramatically after he retired from the Boston Celtics in 1969. He made what he later called "a clean break" from his life in Boston and moved back to the West Coast, settling in Los Angeles. Although he had been well paid by the Celtics, he never commanded as high a salary as current basketball stars do, so he began to look for a new line of work. He hired an acting agent and landed a few bit roles on several television series. He also began to give lectures at universities throughout the United States.

Russell greatly enjoyed this opportunity to exchange ideas with America's youth. During the question-and-answer session that followed his speeches, he was usually asked to comment on pressing political issues; but he also fielded questions about his basketball career. At one session in 1970, a student asked Russell why he was considered a better

Back in action in 1973, the newly appointed head coach of the Seattle SuperSonics advises veteran player Dick Snyder. Russell faced the doubly difficult task in Seattle of rebuilding a losing basketball team and rescuing a failing franchise.

player than Wilt Chamberlain, even though Russell's chief rival had compiled much better individual statistics on far inferior teams. Chamberlain, who was never backed by a strong supporting cast, had to be the superior player, the student argued.

Russell pointed out that Chamberlain had at times been surrounded by some very good players, including Elgin Baylor and Jerry West on the 1968–69 Los Angeles Lakers. Then Russell spoke about their final meeting, which had also been his last professional game. With the NBA title on the line, Chamberlain had taken himself out of the contest in the fourth quarter after he had hurt his ankle. The Lakers center's refusal to remain on the court had disappointed Russell; he had wanted to end his career on a high note, matched against his toughest opponent.

A reporter in the audience, hearing Russell's complaint, filed a story that the former Celtics great had called Chamberlain a quitter. The two men had been good friends over the years, despite the media's portrayal of them as archrivals. But with the release of this story, a feud developed between Russell and Chamberlain that took several years to patch up.

In addition to going on the lecture circuit, Russell hosted a radio program appropriately named "The Bill Russell Show" and filled in for Dick Cavett and other well-known personalities as the host on television talk shows. The American public quickly discovered that Russell was really not the way the media often portrayed him; rather than being a glowering, angry person, he was a man of substantial warmth and mirth. He also possessed an extremely infectious laugh.

The nation got to know Russell even better when he launched his career as a basketball analyst in the early 1970s. Off and on for the next 13 years, he offered an expert's knowledge of the game for 3 different networks: ABC, CBS, and TBS. To at least one television critic, the ballplayer-turned-broadcaster always called it as he saw it: "Russell's commentary on . . . NBA games has been as loose, confident, skillful, and precise as his play at center for the Celtics. You know exactly when he's disgusted, exactly when he's bemused, exactly when he's bored."

Russell was never one to hide his feelings. When Red Auerbach wanted to retire his star player's uniform to make sure Russell's number six would not be worn by anyone else on the Celtics, Russell refused to take part in the ceremony. He did not like to be fussed over; he had always played the game for its own pleasures, not for individual honors.

He eventually reached a compromise with Auerbach. In March 1972, Russell arrived at Boston Garden (his first time there since his retirement) to broadcast a Celtics game, only to discover that Auerbach was planning to hold a surprise ceremony for him at halftime. When Russell objected yet again, they resolved to hold the festivities prior to the game, before any of the fans arrived.

Russell ran into a similar problem with the Basketball Hall of Fame. In 1974, he was selected for induction into the Hall. As the first black player to receive this honor, he responded to the announcement by saying he did not want to be enshrined, "for personal reasons." Russell commented later, "I have very little faith in cheers, what they mean and how long they will last, compared with the faith I have in my own love for the game. The Basketball Hall of Fame is the biggest cheer of all." In spite of his protestations, the Hall went ahead and inducted him.

By then, Russell had returned to the NBA circuit. In the spring of 1973, he received a phone call from Sam Schulman, the principle owner of the Seattle SuperSonics, soliciting recommendations for a new coach. "What about you?" Schulman eventually asked Russell.

As a basketball analyst in the 1970s and 1980s, Russell served up outspoken commentary that was fully in keeping with his character. "I never in my life consciously worked to be liked," he once said. "I work only to be respected."

Expressing little desire to become a head coach, Russell gave Schulman an impossibly long list of demands that would have to be met before he agreed to come to Seattle. A few weeks later, Schulman told Russell he could give him everything he had asked for, including the title of general manager and complete control of the club. Russell accepted the offer.

He soon realized that he had taken on more than he had bargained for. The Seattle franchise was in an utter shambles. The team fared miserably on the court and did just as poorly at the box office.

During his first year as coach and general manager, Russell put a lot of energy into publicizing the team. He wanted the franchise to draw more people and gain better television and radio contracts. Then, as soon as the team was well off financially, he intended to sign the kinds of players a team looking to win a championship needed to have on its roster.

Under Russell in 1973–74, the SuperSonics won 10 more games than they had the previous year. The team made the playoffs the year after that, a first for the Seattle franchise. When Russell's squad made the playoffs the next year too, the future began to look even brighter. Not only did the SuperSonics have solid young players such as Dennis Johnson and Fred Brown; Russell had managed to garner four extra first-round draft picks by trading away some of the higher-salaried players on the team's roster.

As good as Russell's plan was, it never panned out. The players bickered with one another when the team lost; they were a far cry from the unselfish Celtics of Russell's heyday. When he tried to be honest with them, his approach backfired. On one occasion, a Seattle player entered Russell's office and asked to be traded; he was convinced that Russell did not like his style of play. When Russell told him the truth—he was trying to trade the player, but no other team wanted him—the person's confidence was shaken, and he did even less to help the team than before.

Around this time, Russell began to consider re-signing from his dual post. He decided to stick it out, however; he was hopeful that the situation would turn around during the 1976–77 season. When it did not, he and the SuperSonics went their separate ways.

On the sidelines once again, Russell had an easy time keeping himself busy. He resumed his role as a broadcaster and continued to give lectures. He wrote a syndicated newspaper column and worked on his second autobiography, *Second Wind*, which he coauthored with future Pulitzer Prize winner Taylor Branch; this widely praised sports memoir was published in 1979, 13 years after the publication of Russell's first autobiography, *Go Up for Glory*.

Russell also resumed his acting career. He made a popular television commercial for the nation's largest telephone company; the advertisement featured him sitting behind an office desk and sinking a shot across the room. He landed an even lengthier starring role on the hit television show "Miami Vice"; in the hour-long episode, he portrayed a financially troubled judge who turns to his son, played by NBA all-star Bernard King, for help.

Russell's home life kept him occupied as well after he married for the second time, wedding Didi Anstett following a seven-year courtship. The marriage revealed that a definite change in Russell's character had taken place over the years. "I have gone through a time of rage when I hated all white people," he noted. "Now I am married to one."

In the spring of 1987, exactly a decade after he left the SuperSonics, Russell became head coach of the Sacramento Kings, with the expectation that he would eventually move up to the front office. His reign as coach was fairly brief, however. When it became apparent in March 1988 that he was too distant from his players, he was moved to another post, executive vice-president in charge of basketball operations. When Russell was dismissed from this job

the following year, he returned to his adopted home of Seattle, where he currently resides.

It is unlikely that Russell will stay away for long from a sport that offers the kinds of challenges he so clearly loves. Anyone who has ever watched him in action has witnessed his undeniable passion for what he called in a 1979 *New York Times Magazine* article the "white heat of competition":

It never started with a hot streak by a single player, or with a breakdown of one team's defense. It usually began when three or four of the ten guys on the floor would heat up; they would be the catalysts, and they were almost always the stars in the league. . . . The feeling would spread to

Serving as a reminder to the Boston players, their opponents, and all basketball fans of the Celtics' winning tradition, Russell's uniform number—6—now hangs with other banners from the Boston Garden rafters, alongside the 11 championship pennants he helped the Celtics win from 1956 to 1969.

the other guys, and we'd all levitate. Then the game would just take off, and there'd be a natural ebb and flow that reminded you of how rhythmic and musical basketball is supposed to be. I'd find myself thinking, "This is it. I want this to keep going," and I'd actually be rooting for the other team. When their players made spectacular moves, I wanted their shots to go into the bucket; that's how pumped up I'd be. I'd be out there talking to the other Celtics, encouraging them and pushing myself harder, but at the same time part of me would be pulling for the other players too.

Win or lose, Bill Russell always relished the challenge of the game. "He told me," his daughter said, "that he never listened to the boos because he never listened to the cheers. He did it for himself."

APPENDIX: CAREER STATISTICS

REGULAR SEASON RECORD WITH THE BOSTON CELTICS

YEAR	G	MIN	FGA	FGM	FG PCT	FTA	FTM	FT PCT	REB	REB AVG	ASST	PTS	AVG
1956–57	48	1,695	649	277	.427	309	152	.492	943	19.6	88	706	14.7
1957–58	69	2,640	1,032	456	.442	443	230	.519	1,564	22.7	202	1,142	16.6
1958–59	70	2,979	997	456	.457	428	256	.598	1,612	23.0	222	1,168	16.7
1959–60	74	3,146	1,189	555	.467	392	240	.612	1,778	24.0	277	1,350	18.2
1960–61	78	3,458	1,250	532	.426	469	258	.550	1,868	23.9	264	1,322	16.9
1961–62	76	3,433	1,258	575	.457	481	286	.594	1,891	24.9	341	1,436	18.9
1962–63	78	3,500	1,182	511	.432	517	287	.555	1,843	23.6	348	1,309	16.8
1963–64	78	3,482	1,077	466	.433	429	236	.550	1,930	24.7	370	1,168	15.0
1964–65	78	3,466	980	429	.438	426	244	.573	1,878	24.1	410	1,102	14.1
1965–66	78	3,386	943	391	.415	405	223	.551	1,779	22.8	221	1,005	12.9
1966–67	81	3,297	870	395	.454	467	285	.610	1,700	21.0	258	1,075	13.5
1967–68	78	2.953	858	365	.425	460	247	.537	1,451	18.6	242	977	12.5
1968–69	77	3,291	645	279	.433	388	204	.526	1,484	19.3	231	762	9.9
Totals	963	40,726	12,930	5,687	.440	5,614	3,148	.561	21,721	22.6	4,096	14,522	15.1

PLAYOFF RECORD WITH THE BOSTON CELTICS

YEAR	G	MIN	FGA	FGM	FG PCT	FTA	FTM	FT PCT	REB	REB AVG	ASST	PTS	AVG
1956–69	165	7,497	2,335	1,003	.430	1,106	667	.603	4,104	24.9	770	2,673	16.2

ALL-STAR GAME RECORD

YEAR	G	MIN	FGA	FGM	FG PCT	FTA	FTM	FT PCT	REB	REB AVG	ASST	PTS	AVG
1957–69	12	343	111	51	.459	34	18	.529	139	11.6	39	120	10.0

CHRONOLOGY

—————— ❦ ——————

1934	Born William Felton Russell on February 12 in Monroe, Louisiana
1943	Moves to Oakland, California; takes up the sport of basketball
1952	Graduates from McClymonds High School; tours the Pacific Northwest with a team of California high school all-stars; wins a scholarship to the University of San Francisco (USF)
1955	Leads the USF Dons to the National Collegiate Athletic Association (NCAA) championship; named the NCAA tournament's most valuable player
1956	Ends college basketball career with a 55-game winning streak while leading the USF Dons to their second straight national championship; rejects offer to play with the Harlem Globetrotters; leads the U.S. Olympic basketball team to a gold medal in the Summer Games; marries Rose Swisher; joins the Boston Celtics
1957	Helps the Celtics claim their first National Basketball Association (NBA) championship
1958	Wins the first of four rebounding titles and the first of five Most Valuable Player Awards
1959	Leads the Celtics to the first of eight straight NBA championships; travels to Africa on behalf of the U.S. State Department
1963	Voted for the first time to the all-NBA team; takes part in the March on Washington for Jobs and Freedom
1966	Appointed head coach of the Celtics; *Go Up for Glory* is published
1969	Retires as player-coach of the Celtics
1973	Appointed head coach and general manager of the Seattle SuperSonics
1974	Inducted into the Basketball Hall of Fame
1977	Resigns from position with the Seattle SuperSonics; marries Didi Anstett
1979	*Second Wind* is published
1987	Russell becomes head coach of the Sacramento Kings
1988	Named vice-president in charge of basketball operations of the Kings
1989	Dismissed from position with the Kings

FURTHER READING

———— ❦ ————

Auerbach, Red, and Joe Fitzgerald. *On and off the Court.* New York: Macmillan, 1985.

Axthelm, Pete. *The City Game: Basketball from the Garden to the Playground.* New York: Penguin, 1982.

Chamberlain, Wilt, and David Shaw. *Wilt: Just Like Any Other 7-foot Black Millionaire Who Lives Next Door.* New York: Macmillan, 1973.

Clary, Jack. *Basketball's Great Moments.* New York: McGraw-Hill, 1988.

Cousy, Robert. *Basketball Is My Life, as Told to Al Hirshberg.* Englewood Cliffs, NJ: Prentice-Hall, 1958.

Heinsohn, Tommy, and Joe Fitzgerald. *Give 'em the Hook.* Englewood Cliffs, NJ: Prentice-Hall, 1988.

Hollander, Zander, and Alex Sachare. *The Official NBA Basketball Encyclopedia.* New York: New American Library, 1989.

Packer, Billy, with Roland Lazenby. *College Basketball's 25 Greatest Teams.* St. Louis, MO: The Sporting News Book Publishing, 1989.

————. *Hoops!* Chicago, IL: Contemporary Books, Inc., 1985.

Russell, Bill, and Taylor Branch. *Second Wind: Memoirs of an Opinionated Man.* New York: Random House, 1979.

Russell, Bill, with William McSweeney. *Go Up for Glory.* New York: Coward-McCann, 1966.

Russell, Karen K. "Growing Up with Privilege and Prejudice." *The New York Times Magazine,* June 14, 1987.

Ryan, Bob, and Dick Raphael. *The Boston Celtics.* New York: Addison-Wesley, 1989.

INDEX

"Miami Vice," 103
Minneapolis Lakers, 69, 71, 72, 75. *See also* Los Angeles Lakers
Monroe, Louisiana, 21, 23, 29
Montreal Canadiens, 21
Most, Johnny, 84
Mullen, Jerry, 44, 49

Naulls, Willie, 44
NBA's Official Encyclopedia of Pro Basketball, The, 62
Nelson, Don, 13, 18
Newell, Pete, 51
New York Knickerbockers, 76, 90, 93, 96
New York Times, 12, 16
New York Times Magazine, 91, 104
New York Yankees, 21
Nichols, Jack, 61

Oakland, California, 26, 28, 29, 31, 34, 37, 38, 55
Olympic Games, 54–55
Oregon State University, 44, 45
Ouachita River, 23

Perry, Hal, 44
Pettit, Bob, 62, 63, 75
Philadelphia 76ers, 11, 12–13, 16–17, 83–84, 86, 90, 92, 93, 96
Philadelphia Warriors, 60, 62, 65–66, 74–75, 76, 82. *See also* San Francisco Warriors
Phillip, Andy, 61
Powles, George, 32, 33

Ramsey, Frank, 61, 71, 81
Reading, Massachusetts, 65
Reed, Willis, 93
Risen, Arnie, 59, 60
Robertson, Oscar, 14, 75, 77, 82
Rochester Royals, 56, 57
Russell, Bill, Jr. (son), 65
Russell, Charlie (brother), 24, 25, 29, 30, 32
Russell, Charlie (father), 24, 25–26, 28, 29–30, 37, 39,

49, 80, 92
Russell, Jacob (son), 65
Russell, Karen (daughter), 65, 91, 105
Russell, Katie (mother), 24, 25, 28–29, 30
Russell, Old Man (grandfather), 24, 80, 92, 94
Russell, William Felton "Bill"
  birth, 23
  with Boston Celtics, 11–15, 16, 17–18, 19, 20–21, 55, 57, 59–67, 69–72, 74, 75, 77, 80–82, 84–87, 89–90, 92–97
  as broadcaster, 100–101
  divorce, 94
  drafted by Celtics, 54–57
  early life, 24–32
  fights racial prejudice, 79–80, 90–91
  as head coach of Kings, 103
  as head coach of SuperSonics, 102–3
  in high school, 32–35, 38
  on lecture circuit, 100
  marriage, 55, 103
  named coach of Celtics, 86
  receives scholarship to USF, 39
  retires from Celtics, 99
  tours Latin America, 49, 54
  travels in Africa, 72
  with U.S. Olympic basketball team, 21, 52–55
  with USF Dons, 21, 38–47, 39–47, 49–52
  wins first MVP Award, 67
  wins first NBA title, 62–63
  wins first NCAA title, 47
Ruth, Babe, 21

Sacramento Kings, 103
St. Louis Hawks, 56, 62–63, 65, 66–67, 71, 75, 82, 92
Sanders, Thomas "Satch," 13, 74, 81, 95
San Francisco Naval Yard, 37
San Francisco Warriors, 13, 17, 90
Saperstein, Abe, 53, 72

Schayes, Dolph, 60, 71
Schulman, Sam, 101, 102
Seattle SuperSonics, 101–3
Seattle University, 69
Second Wind, 14, 24, 25, 31, 42, 64, 90, 103
Selvy, Frank, 77
Sharman, Bill, 60, 71
Siegfried, Larry, 13
Southern Methodist University, 52
Sports Illustrated, 12, 16, 20
State Department, U.S., 49, 72
Swegle, Brick, 33, 34
Swisher, Rose (first wife), 49, 55, 65, 94
Syracuse Nationals, 60, 62, 65, 71, 75, 82. *See also* Philadelphia 76ers

Taylor Methodist Church, 55
Thurmond, Nate, 13, 82, 95
Tomsic, Ronald, 54
Treu, Bill, 34, 35

U.S. Olympic basketball team, 53, 54–55
University of California at Berkeley, 51
University of California at Los Angeles (UCLA), Bruins, 21, 42, 44, 51, 52
University of Colorado, 46
University of Kansas, 74
University of San Francisco (USF) Dons, 21, 38, 42, 43, 44–47, 49–52
University of Utah, 52

Walker, Chet, 84
Walsh, James, 54
Walton, Bill, 52
Washington, Kermit, 52
Washington, D.C., 49, 69
West, Jerry, 11, 17, 18, 75, 77, 96–97, 100
Wooden, John, 21
Woolpert, Phil, 38, 43, 44, 49, 51

Yardley, George, 71

PICTURE CREDITS

MILES SHAPIRO is a Yale University graduate whose short stories, essays, and book reviews have appeared in various publications. A native of Washington, D.C., he currently resides in Brooklyn, New York.

NATHAN IRVIN HUGGINS is W.E.B. Du Bois Professor of History and Director of the W.E.B. Du Bois Institute for Afro-American Research at Harvard University. He previously taught at Columbia University. Professor Huggins is the author of numerous books, including *Black Odyssey: The Afro-American Ordeal in Slavery*, *The Harlem Renaissance*, and *Slave and Citizen: The Life of Frederick Douglass*.